Contents

M000166845

Introduction

Castles and fortified houses can be found all over England. Impressive, oppressive, dramatic, romantic; but who built these castles, and why?

This book provides a guide to nearly 150 of England's fortified structures, said to date from the Iron Age (such as Maiden Castle) right up the 1930s (Castle Drogo). These structures have been included due to the significance of their surviving architecture or their prominent place in the history of England (or both!). Nearly all are open to the public in some form or can still be viewed externally.

Many fortified sites started life as Iron Age forts, built as defensive positions against warring tribes or invaders. These were often built on high ground with commanding views over the surrounding countryside and consisted of a series of ramparts and ditches. One of the most famous Iron Age fortifications is Maiden Castle near Dorchester in Dorset.

After the Roman invasion, some hill forts were occupied by the Romans whilst others were destroyed or abandoned but reoccupied later as refuges against Anglo-Saxon invaders. From the 8th century onwards, the Anglo-Saxons would also reoccupy hillforts as defensive sites against Viking invaders.

The arrival of the Normans in 1066 led to a new age of castle construction and quite literally changed the landscape of England. Initially the sites chosen for Norman fortresses were in populous towns and villages. Later castles often reused ancient hill fort sites, as their situations were still as relevant for the Normans as they had been for Iron Age people. The Normans also saw the merit of controlling the Roman road networks, which were still the main routes through the countryside, and so some castles were constructed at strategic points such as river crossings and crossroads.

The first Norman castles were motte-and-bailey castles, comprising a wooden or stone fortified tower, called a keep, set on an artificial mound, called a motte, surrounded by a walled courtyard (the bailey). These fortifications were relatively easy and fast to construct. The remains of many of these castles can be found throughout the countryside, mostly consisting of just the motte, bailey and ditches. Some stone-built motte-and-bailey castles have survived intact; examples include the Tower of London and Windsor Castle, the latter being the largest inhabited castle in the world and the oldest in continuous occupation, having been a royal residence to 39 monarchs for over 900 years.

The motte-and-bailey castle design began to fall out of favour in the 13th century as more and more castles started being built in stone. Unique to the English and Scottish border areas at this time were stone pele towers, built as both a watch tower and refuge from attack during the troubled Scottish Marches era. The towers were surrounded by an enclosed courtyard or bailey. This in turn was surrounded by a palisade (a defensive wall), with a protective ditch dug on the other side.

From the 14th century onwards, castles also began to combine their defensive role with that of a fine residence or palace.

In the Tudor period when Henry VIII's break with the Catholic Church meant the threat of invasion was high, he had a series of castles built along the coast from Cornwall to Kent. Portland Castle in Dorset, Pendennis Castle and St Mawes Castle in Cornwall, Calshot Castle in Hampshire and Deal Castle and Walmer Castle in Kent are some of the finest examples of these fortifications.

In 1642 with the outbreak of the English Civil War between Parliamentarians ('Roundheads') and Royalists ('Cavaliers') many castles were brought back into use. It soon became clear that medieval castles would be vulnerable to the new siege weapon of choice; the cannon. Existing defences were renovated and walls 'countermured', or backed by earth, to protect them from cannon fire. After the Civil War, many castles were 'slighted' or destroyed and castle building declined as peace returned.

One of the best examples of how a castle can develop throughout the ages is Dover Castle in Kent. Originally an Iron Age hill fort, it still houses a Roman lighthouse and an Anglo-Saxon church, which was probably part of a Saxon fortified settlement. After his victory at the Battle of Hastings in 1066, William the Conqueror strengthened the defences with a Norman earthwork and timber-stockaded castle. In use as a garrison from the time of the Norman invasion until 1958, tunnels were dug under the castle in the late 18th century. During the Second World War these same tunnels were used as the headquarters from which the Dunkirk evacuation was masterminded.

Most castles featured in this book are open to visitors, even if this is in the form of accommodation or a tourist attraction. However, some remain privately owned and their inclusion in the book does not imply a right of public access. Castles owned or managed by English Heritage and National Trust are generally open to the public at some point throughout the year although opening, closing and site accessibility details are subject to change. It is always advisable to check with the specific attraction in advance. Telephone number and website, where available, are listed in the property description.

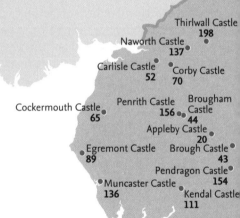

Northern England

Scotland

Irish Sea

Thirlwall Castle
198

Naworth Castle
137

Carlisle Castle
52

Corby Castle
70

Cockermouth Castle
65

Penrith Castle
156

Brougham Castle
44

Appleby Castle
20

Egremont Castle
89

Brough Castle
43

Pendragon Castle
154

Muncaster Castle
136

Kendal Castle
111

Dalton Castle
72

Lancaster Castl
118

Piel Castle
162

Clitheroe Castle
62

Berwick Castle **36**

Norham Castle **142**

Lindisfarne Castle **126**

tal Castle Bamburgh Castle **26**
•0

Chillingham Castle **57**

Dunstanburgh Castle **84**

Alnwick Castle **18**

Edlingham Warkworth Castle
Castle **210**
88

Mitford Castle **135**

Belsay Castle **31**

Aydon Castle **24** Tynemouth Castle **207**

Newcastle Castle Keep **140**

Prudhoe
Castle Hylton Castle
170 **110**

Durham Castle
86

England

Raby Castle **171**

Barnard Castle **28**

Richmond Castle **174**

Bolton Castle **41** Helmsley Castle Scarborough Castle **189**
Middleham Castle **106** Pickering Castle **160**
134

Knaresborough Castle
116

Skipton Castle Spofforth Castle
•**193** **194**

Pontefract Castle
163

Sandal Castle
188

Numbers in **bold** indicate the page
where the property can be found

North Sea

Central England

Clitheroe Castle
62

Pontefract Castle
163

Sandal Castle
188

Irish
Sea

Conisbrough Castle
68

Halton Castle
101

Peveril Castle
158

Bolsover Castle
40

Chester Castle
56

Beeston Castle
30

Newark Castle
138

Whittington Castle
215

Tutbury Castle
206

England

Wales

Shrewsbury Castle
192

Ashby de la Zouch
Castle
23

Acton Burnell Castle
16

Tamworth Castle
196

Kirby Muxloe
Castle 115

Clun Castle
64

Kenilworth Castle
112

Ludlow Castle
129

Wigmore Castle
216

Warwick Castle
212

Clifford Castle
61

Deddington Castle
79

Wilton Castle
217

Goodrich Castle
98

Oxford Castle
152

St Briavels Castle
180

Berkeley Castle
32

Numbers in **bold** indicate the page
where the property can be found

North Sea

Lincoln Castle
124

Baconsthorpe Castle
25

Castle Rising
55

Castle Acre Castle
53

Caister Castle
45

Norwich Castle
143

Fotheringhay Castle
96

Kimbolton Castle
114

Framlingham Castle
97

Clare Castle
60

Orford Castle
150

Hedingham Castle
104

Colchester Castle
66

Berkhamsted Castle
34

Southern England

Clun Castle
64

Ludlow Castle
129

Wigmore Castle
216

Kenilworth Castle
112

Warwick Castle
212

Clifford Castle
61

Wilton Castle
217

Deddington Castle
79

Goodrich Castle
98

Wales

St Briavels Castle
180

Berkeley Castle
32

Oxford Castle
152

Thornbury Castle
199

Donnington Cast
80

Farleigh Hungerford Castle
93

Ludgershall Castle
128

Nunney Castle
144

Farnham Castle Keep
94

Dunster Castle
85

Old Sarum
148

Old Wardour Castle
149

Winchester Castle
218

Wolvesey Castle
222

Sherborne Old Castle
191

Portchester Castle
164

Calshot Castle
46

Christchurch Castle
58

Maiden Castle
132

Hurst Castle
109

Powderham Castle
168

Carisbrooke Cast
and Museum
50

Portland Castle
166

Corfe Castle
71

Rufus Castle
178

Kimbolton Castle
114

Framlingham Castle
97

Clare Castle
60

Orford Castle
150

n g l a n d

Hedingham Castle
104

Colchester Castle
66

Berkhamsted Castle
34

North Sea

Hadleigh Castle
100

Tower of London
204

Cooling Castle **69**

Windsor Castle
220

Rochester Castle
176

Upnor Castle
208

Eynsford Castle
92

Canterbury Castle
48 74

Dane John Mound

Leeds Castle
120

Deal Castle **78**

Tonbridge Castle
202

Walmer Castle **209**

Sutton Valence Castle
195

Hever Castle
108

Dover Castle **82**

Scotney Castle
190

Westenhanger Castle
214

Bodiam Castle
38

Bramber
Castle
42

Herstmonceux
Castle
107

Rye Castle **179**
Camber Castle **47**

Lewes
Castle
122

Hastings Castle **102**

Arundel Castle
22

Pevensey Castle
157

English Channel

Numbers in **bold** indicate the page
where the property can be found

Southwest England

Numbers in **bold** indicate the page
where the property can be found

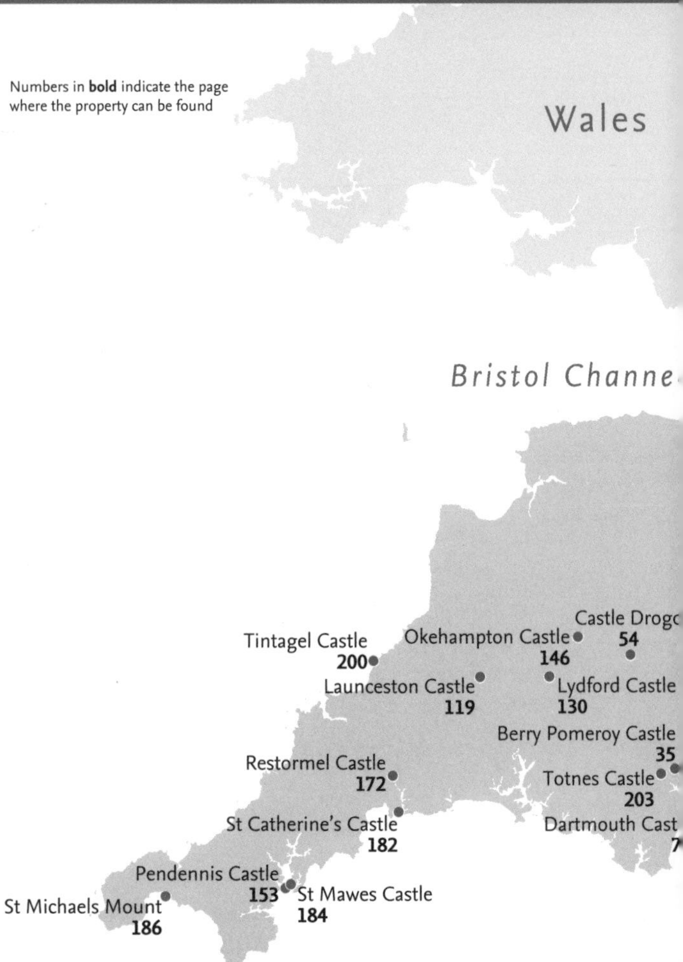

Wales

Bristol Channe

Clifford Castle
61

Deddington Castle
79

Wilton Castle
217

Goodrich Castle
98

St Briavels Castle
180

Berkeley Castle
32

Oxford Castle
152

Thornbury Castle
199

Donnington Castle
80

Farleigh Hungerford Castle
93

Ludgershall Castle
128

Farnham Castle Keep
94

Nunney Castle
144

Old Sarum
148

Dunster Castle
85

England   Old Wardour Castle
149

Winchester Castle
218

Wolvesey Castle
222

Sherborne Old Castle
191

Portchester Castle
164

Calshot Castle
46

Maiden Castle
132

Christchurch Castle
58

Hurst Castle
109

Powderham Castle
168

Portland Castle
166

Corfe Castle
71

Carisbrooke Castle
and Museum
50

Rufus Castle
178

English Channel

Acton Burnell Castle, Shropshire

Acton Burnell, Shrewsbury, Shropshire, SY5 7PE
0370 333 1181 | www.english-heritage.org.uk

OWNED BY ENGLISH HERITAGE

The extensive remains of a fortified tower house. Built between 1284–1293 by Robert Burnell, Bishop of Bath and Wells, friend and advisor to King Edward I, the location of the manor house was important, close to the old Roman road of Watling Street. The influence of Bishop Burnell was such that this little Shropshire village twice hosted the English Parliament, first in 1283 and again in 1285. This initial meeting in 1283 is particularly important as it was the first time in English history that the Commons were fully represented. The meeting also resulted in the Statute of Acton Burnell, a law that gave protection to creditors, showing how important trade and traders were at the time. Only the shell of the former residence remains open to the public.

Alnwick Castle, Northumberland

Alnwick Castle, Alnwick, Northumberland, NE66 1NQ
01665 511 100 | www.alnwickcastle.com

OWNED BY THE DUKE OF NORTHUMBERLAND

Medieval castle and stately home. Built following the Norman Conquest and renovated and remodelled many times since then, it is the great northern fortress of the powerful Percy family, the Dukes of Northumberland. The interiors of the rooms have also been remodelled over the centuries, most notably by architect Robert Adam in the 18th century.

The son of the 1st East of Northumberland, who was born in the castle, was known as Harry Hotspur due to his hot-headedness in battle, and he was the inspiration for Hotspur in the Shakespeare's *King Henry IV (Part 1)*. In recent years, Alnwick Castle is perhaps best known as 'Hogwarts' in the first two *Harry Potter* films. However, Alnwick is not just limited to the castle, with the renowned Alnwick Garden also open to the public.

Appleby Castle, Cumbria

Appleby Castle, Appleby-in-Westmorland, Cumbria, CA16 6XH

017683 30318 | www.applebycastle.co.uk/AC

OWNED BY MRS SALLY NIGHTINGALE

An intact Norman castle and mansion house. Standing guard over the Eden Valley since Norman times, the castle was once owned by the Kings of England. Built when King William II took Westmorland from the Scots, the great castle keep, known as Caesar's Tower, dates from around 1170.

Arundel Castle, West Sussex

Arundel Castle & Gardens, Arundel, West Sussex,
BN18 9AB
01903 882173 | www.arundelcastle.org

OWNED BY ARUNDEL CASTLE TRUST

A restored medieval castle, founded by Roger de
Montgomery in 1067. The castle was damaged during
the English Civil War and restored throughout the 18th
and 19th centuries, when it became one of the first
English stately homes to be fitted with electric lights and
central heating. The castle has been the hereditary stately
home of the Duke of Norfolk for over 400 years. Most of
the castle and grounds are open to the public; entrance
charges apply to both the castle and gardens.

Ashby de la Zouch Castle, Leicestershire

South Street, Ashby de la Zouch, Leicestershire, LE65 1BR
01530 413343 | www.english-heritage.org.uk

OWNED BY ENGLISH HERITAGE

Formerly a fortified manor house dating back to the 11th century, the castle takes its name from Ashby's first Norman Lord, Alain de Parrhoet la Souche. However, it was not until the 15th century when Edward IV granted the house and land to his chancellor William, Lord Hastings, that an impressive transformation from manor house to castle (and principle seat of Lord Hastings) took place. Sadly, the castle was all but destroyed in the 17th century in the aftermath of the English Civil War, although visitors can still climb the impressive Hastings Tower and discover the underground passage with messages from centuries past.

Aydon Castle, Northumberland

Off Aydon Road, Corbridge, Northumberland, NE45 5PJ
01434 632450 | www.english-heritage.org.uk

OWNED BY ENGLISH HERITAGE

An intact 13th-century English manor house, also known
as Aydon Hall. Originally built as an undefended manor
house, it was fortified at the outbreak of Anglo-Scottish
Wars. However, the castle was captured by the Scots in
1315, seized by English rebels two years later, and then
once again occupied by the Scots in 1346. The castle
was converted into a farm in the 17th century and
remained as such until 1966 when it was restored to its
medieval appearance.

Sebastien Coell / shutterstock.com

Baconsthorpe Castle, Norfolk

Hall Lane, Baconsthorpe, Norfolk, NR25 9LN
0370 333 1181 | www.english-heritage.org.uk

OWNED BY ENGLISH HERITAGE

The ruins of a moated and fortified 15th-century manor house. Built by the ambitious Heydon family between 1460–1486 as a simple manor house, it was later fortified and enlarged as the family's wealth grew. After the English Civil War, the house fell into ruin. However, it remained as a private residence until the 1920s.

Bamburgh Castle, Northumberland

Bamburgh, Northumberland, NE69 7DF
01668 214515 | www.bamburghcastle.com

OWNED BY THE ARMSTRONG FAMILY

An intact and inhabited Norman castle. Once the Royal
Seat of the Kings of Northumbria, the first written
reference to the castle dates from AD 547 when it was
captured by the Anglo-Saxon ruler Ida of Bernicia.
Vikings destroyed the original fortification in AD 993.
The Normans built a new castle on the site, which forms
the core of the current structure. Open to the public,
entrance charges apply.

Barnard Castle, County Durham

Scar Top, Barnard Castle, Durham, DL12 8PR
01833 638212 | www.english-heritage.org.uk

OWNED BY ENGLISH HERITAGE

The remains of a medieval castle. Founded by the Normans shortly after the Conquest, the castle enjoyed its heyday under Bernard de Bailliol during the latter half of the 12th century. The castle passed into the possession of Richard Neville, Earl of Warwick, and then to King Richard III, falling into ruins in the century after his death.

Beeston Castle, Tarporley, Cheshire

Chapel Lane, Beeston, Cheshire, CW6 9TX
01829 260464 | www.english-heritage.org.uk

OWNED BY ENGLISH HERITAGE

The ruined remains of a 13th-century castle. Standing on a rocky crag high above the Cheshire Plain, Beeston Castle was built in the 1220s by Ranulf de Blondeville, 6th Earl of Chester, on his return from the Crusades. The castle remained in good repair until the 16th century, when it was considered to be of no further strategic importance. It was partially demolished in 1646, in accordance with Oliver Cromwell's destruction order, to prevent its further use as a stronghold. Treasure belonging to Richard II is rumoured to be hidden in the castle grounds.

Belsay Castle, Northumberland

Belsay, near Morpeth, Northumberland, NE20 0DX
01661 881636 | www.english-heritage.org.uk

OWNED BY THE MIDDLETON FAMILY
UNDER THE GUARDIANSHIP OF ENGLISH HERITAGE

The remains of a medieval castle. This substantial,
three-storey rectangular pele tower with turrets and
battlements was constructed around 1370. Home to the
Middleton family for more than seven centuries, a new
manor house was added to the tower in 1614 with a
garden created to link the two structures. The family
remained resident at the manor house until 1962, after
which it came under the guardianship of English
Heritage in 1980.

Berkeley Castle, Gloucestershire

Gloucestershire, GL13 9BQ
01453 810303 | www.berkeley-castle.com

OWNED BY BERKELEY CASTLE CHARITABLE TRUST

Berkeley Castle is the oldest continuously-occupied castle in England after the royal residences. The first castle at the site was a Norman motte-and-bailey structure, built around 1067, shortly after the Conquest. The present castle has remained within the Berkeley family since they reconstructed it in the 12th century. It is also believed to be the scene of the murder of King Edward II in 1327.

Berkhamsted Castle, Hertfordshire

White Hill, Berkhamsted, Hertfordshire, HP4 1LJ
0370 333 1181 | www.english-heritage.org.uk

OWNED BY ENGLISH HERITAGE

The original motte-and-bailey castle was built during the
Norman Conquest of England to control a key route
between London and the Midlands, having been the site
where the English submitted to William the Conqueror
following his victory at the Battle of Hastings. Extended
in the mid-12th century, the castle was besieged in 1216
during the civil war between King John and rebel barons.
Subsequently used to hold royal prisoners, it was described
as being in ruins by the middle of the 16th century, by which
time much of its stonework had been misappropriated.

Berry Pomeroy Castle, Totnes, Devon

Berry Pomeroy, Totnes, Devon, TQ9 6LJ
01803 866618 | www.english-heritage.org.uk

OWNED BY ENGLISH HERITAGE

The remains of an Elizabethan mansion within the walls
of an earlier 15th-century Tudor castle built by the
Pomeroy family. Intended to become the most spectacular
house in Devon, Sir Edward Seymour started building
his new four-storey house in 1560. Enlarged by his son
from 1600, it was never completed and had been
abandoned by 1700. It is reputed to be one of the most
haunted castles in Britain.

Berwick Castle, Berwick-upon-Tweed, Northumberland

Berwick-upon-Tweed, Northumberland, TD15 1DF
0370 333 1181 | www.english-heritage.org.uk

OWNED BY ENGLISH HERITAGE

The remains of a medieval castle built in the 12th century by the Scottish King David I. In the 13th century the English King Edward I had the castle rebuilt to include substantial walls to protect the town. Both the town and castle changed hands several times over the centuries that followed, as a result of the Anglo-Scottish conflicts. The construction of ramparts around the town in the 16th century rendered the castle obsolete. Much of the remaining structure was demolished when the town's railway station was built. Some of the 13th-century castle and the medieval town walls survive.

Bodiam Castle, Robertsbridge, East Sussex

Bodiam, near Robertsbridge, East Sussex, TN32 5UA
01580830196 | www.nationaltrust.org.uk

OWNED BY NATIONAL TRUST

An almost complete exterior of a 14th-century moated castle. One of Britain's most romantic and picturesque castles, Bodiam was built in 1385 by Sir Edward Dalyngrigge, a former knight of King Edward III, and is said to have been built to defend the area against a potential French invasion during the Hundred Years War.

Bolsover Castle, Derbyshire

Castle Street, Bolsover, Derbyshire, S44 6PR
01246 822844 | www.english-heritage.org.uk

OWNED BY ENGLISH HERITAGE

Built by the Peverel family in the 12th century, Bolsover Castle became Crown property when the family line died out. Following a siege in 1217, it deteriorated into a ruin, and it was not until 1553 that Sir George Talbot rebuilt it for elegant living rather than defence. Slighted (destroyed) during the Civil War, it again fell into a ruinous state. William Cavendish had the castle restored to good order by the time of his death in 1676. In 1946 the Ministry of Works oversaw the restoration and stabilisation of the building, following the effects of mining subsidence from a nearby colliery.

Bolton Castle, North Yorkshire

Near Leyburn, North Yorkshire, DL8 4ET
01969 623981 | www.boltoncastle.co.uk

OWNED BY BARON BOLTON

A largely intact castle built between 1378 and 1399 by
Sir Richard le Scrope, Chancellor to Richard II. Mary,
Queen of Scots, was held at the castle following her
defeat at the Battle of Langside in 1568. Mary, along
with her retinue of 51 knights, servants and ladies-in-
waiting, stayed in apartments in the south-west tower.
Free to wander the grounds, she often went hunting.
It was here that she also learned to speak English, as she
previously only spoke French and Latin.

Bramber Castle, West Sussex

Castle Lane, Bramber Castle, Bramber, West Sussex,
BN44 3WE
0370 333 1181 | www.english-heritage.org.uk

OWNED BY ENGLISH HERITAGE

This early Norman motte-and-bailey castle was built by
William de Braose around 1075, and remained in the
ownership of the de Braose family for over 250 years. It
was besieged by Parliamentary forces during the English
Civil War, when cannons set up in the nearby church
fired down onto the castle. Today, only the ruins of the
gatehouse survive.

Brough Castle, Church Brough, Cumbria

Church Brough, Cumbria, CA17 4EJ
0370 333 1181 | www.english-heritage.org.uk

OWNED BY ENGLISH HERITAGE

Standing on a ridge commanding the strategic
Stainmore Pass, a key route though the Pennine
mountains, William Rufus first constructed a wooden
motte-and-bailey castle here around 1092 within the old
Roman fort of Verterae. Attacked and destroyed by the
Scots in 1174, it was later rebuilt using stone with the
addition of a square keep. The castle perimeter walls still
stand to a good height in several places, whilst Clifford's
Tower and the keep are both in evidence.

Brougham Castle, near Penrith, Cumbria

Moor Lane, Penrith, Cumbria, CA10 2AA
01768 862488 | www.english-heritage.org.uk

OWNED BY ENGLISH HERITAGE

Brougham Castle was built by Robert de Vieuxpont in the
early 13th century on the site of an earlier Roman fort and
sits on the banks of the River Eamont. With the outbreak
of the Anglo-Scottish Wars in 1296, Brougham became
an important military base and the castle's wooden
defences were replaced with stone walls and a large
stone gatehouse. Such was the importance of Brougham
that Edward I, Hammer of the Scots, visited in 1300.

Caister Castle, Caister-on-Sea, Norfolk

Castle Lane, Caister-on-Sea, Great Yarmouth, Norfolk, NR30 5SN
01664 567707 | www.caistercastle.co.uk

OWNED BY CAISTER CASTLE TRUST

The remains of a 15th-century brick-built castle, surrounded by a moat. The castle was built by Sir John Fastolf (Shakespeare's Falstaff), between 1432 and 1446, and includes a 100ft tower. The castle suffered major damage in 1469, when it was besieged and captured by the Duke of Norfolk. The castle fell into disrepair in the 17th century, when a new house was built nearby. The castle's tower remains intact and can be climbed by visitors.

Calshot Castle, Hampshire

Calshot Road, Calshot, Hampshire, SO45 1BR
02380 892023 (when castle is closed, call
02380 892077) | www.english-heritage.org.uk

OWNED BY ENGLISH HERITAGE

An intact coastal artillery fort, built by Henry VIII to guard
the entrance to Southampton Water. Calshot was built as
part of a chain of defences to protect England's coast
from foreign invasion, following Henry's decision to
break from the Roman Catholic Church. This circular
blockhouse was built in 1540 re-using stone, with a twist
of irony, from Beaulieu Abbey.

Camber Castle, Rye, East Sussex

Harbour Road, Rye, East Sussex, TN31 7TD
01797 227784 | www.english-heritage.org.uk

OWNED BY ENGLISH HERITAGE

The ruin of an artillery fort, built by Henry VIII to guard
the port of Rye. Like Calshot Castle, Camber was built as
a link in the chain of coastal defences to protect England
from foreign invasion, following Henry's decision to
break from the Roman Catholic Church. The circular
tower was built between 1512–1514 and expanded
between 1539–1544. By the end of the 16th century the
silting of the Camber made the castle obsolete.

Canterbury Castle, Canterbury, Kent

Castle Street, Canterbury, Kent, CT1 2PR

OWNED BY CANTERBURY CITY COUNCIL

Shortly after Canterbury submitted to William the Conqueror in October 1066, a simple motte-and-bailey structure was erected. One of the three royal castles of Kent, the motte is still visible as the mound in Dane John Gardens, a corruption of the French word 'donjon', or keep. Construction of the great stone keep took place between 1086–1120. However, after Henry II built his new castle at Dover, Canterbury Castle declined in importance and became the county gaol. By the 17th century it had fallen into ruin, which was further exacerbated in the 19th century by its use as a storage facility by the Canterbury Gas Light and Coke Company. Canterbury City Council purchased the castle in 1928 and have restored the ruins to their current condition.

Carisbrooke Castle and Museum, near Newport, Isle of Wight

Castle Hill, Newport, Isle of Wight, PO30 1XY
01983 522107 | www.english-heritage.org.uk

OWNED BY ENGLISH HERITAGE

Although there has been a fortress on this site since Saxon times and at least AD 544, the present stone Norman motte-and-bailey castle was started around 1100. Carisbrooke experienced its only serious action in 1377, when it was unsuccessfully attacked by a French raiding force. Following his defeat in the English Civil War, King Charles I was imprisoned at the castle for fourteen months before his execution in 1649. His attempt to escape failed after he became wedged in the window bars.

Carlisle Castle, Cumbria

Castle Way, Carlisle, Cumbria, CA3 8UR
01228 591922 | www.english-heritage.org.uk

OWNED BY ENGLISH HERITAGE

Given its strategic location on the English border with
Scotland, it is not surprising that Carlisle Castle is the
most besieged place in the British Isles. The castle was
started during the reign of William II of England, the
son of the Conqueror, at which time Cumberland was
considered a part of Scotland. After driving the Scots
out, William II claimed the region for England and in
1093 a wooden Norman motte-and-bailey castle was
built on the site of an earlier Roman fort. In 1122, Henry
I ordered a stone keep to be constructed; the city walls
also date from this time. Carlisle and her castle changed
hands many times over the next 700 years.

Castle Acre Castle, near Swaffham, Norfolk

Castle Acre, King's Lynn, Norfolk, PE32 2XD
01760 755394 | www.english-heritage.org.uk

OWNED BY ENGLISH HERITAGE

The original Castle Acre Castle was built soon after the Norman Conquest of 1066 by William de Warenne, the first Earl of Surrey. Monks lived at the castle site between 1081 and 1085. In 1089 de Warenne's son gave them a new site where the Castle Acre Priory was built. Much of the site was demolished as a result of Henry VIII's suppression of the monasteries in the 1530s. In 1615 Sir Edward Coke took ownership of the castle and it remains in his family today.

Castle Drogo, Devon

Drewsteignton, near Exeter, Devon, EX6 6PB
01647 433306 | www.nationaltrust.org.uk

OWNED BY NATIONAL TRUST

A country house and castle near Exeter that has the
unique distinction of being the last castle to be built in
England. Castle Drogo was commissioned by Julius Drewe,
the retail entrepreneur who established 'The Home and
Colonial Stores', which made him a millionaire by the
age of 33. Building work began on this entirely granite
structure in 1911, although the outbreak of the First
World War and the Great Depression delayed the project
somewhat and the castle was not completed until 1930,
a year before Drewe passed away. Drewe's grandson and
great-grandson gave the property to the National Trust
in 1974.

Castle Rising, Kings Lynn, Norfolk

Castle Rising, Kings Lynn, Norfolk, PE31 6AH
01553 631330 | www.castlerising.co.uk

**OWNED BY LORD HOWARD OF RISING
(ENGLISH HERITAGE LISTED)**

A well preserved 12th-century castle and earthwork
defences. Built in around 1138 by William d'Aubigny,
1st Earl of Arundel, the castle has served as a hunting
lodge, royal residence and a royal mint. Between 1330–
1358 it was the residence of the exiled former queen
Isabella of France, widow of the murdered Edward II,
who died here. One of the most famous 12th-century
castles in England, the well-preserved stone keep is
amongst the finest surviving examples of its kind and is
surrounded by 12 acres of earthwork defences. Its current
owner, Lord Howard of Rising, is a descendant of
William d'Aubigny.

Chester Castle: Agricola Tower, Chester, Cheshire

Grosvenor Street, Chester, Cheshire, CH1 2DN
0370 333 1181 | www.english-heritage.org.uk

OWNED BY ENGLISH HERITAGE

This 12th-century tower is the only surviving part of
medieval Chester Castle. Built by William the Conqueror
in 1070, the castle became the administrative centre of
the Earldom of Chester. The original wooden motte-and-
bailey castle was rebuilt in stone in the 12th century
along with the outer bailey. The stone gateway to the
inner bailey was also added; this is now known as the
Agricola Tower. The remainder of the castle was
destroyed by fire in the late 18th century.

Chillingham Castle, Northumberland

Chillingham, Alnwick, Northumberland, NE66 5NJ
01668 215359 | www.chillingham-castle.com

OWNED BY SIR HUMPHRY WAKEFIELD

An intact medieval castle. Built in the 12th century as a monastery, Chillingham has been home to the Grey family and their descendants since 1246. King Edward I visited the castle in 1298 whilst on his way north to confront William Wallace in battle. Chillingham became a fully fortified castle in 1344, complete with dungeons and torture chambers. At its centre is the Great Hall, an Elizabethan chamber overlooked by a medieval minstrels gallery.

Christchurch Castle, Dorset

High Street, Christchurch, Dorset, BH23 1AS
0370 333 1181 | www.english-heritage.org.uk

OWNED BY ENGLISH HERITAGE

The remains of a 12th-century castle and lord's house.
Standing on the site of an earlier Saxon fort dating from
around AD 924, the original Norman wooden motte-
and-bailey castle was replaced with a stone keep in 1160.
Also dating from this time is the nearby domestic
Norman dwelling known as the Norman's House, which
was built inside the original castle bailey. Containing the
lord's private apartments, it is the only building that
has survived.

Clare Castle, Suffolk

Malting Lane, Clare, Sudbury, Suffolk, CO10 8NW
01787 277731 | www.clarecastlecountrypark.co.uk

OWNED BY CLARE TOWN COUNCIL

A motte-and-bailey castle was built here shortly after the
Norman Conquest by Richard Fitz Gilbert, cousin of
William the Conqueror. It was the de Clare family that
replaced that first wooden structure with a stone keep
in the 13th century, and later the castle became the
home of Elizabeth de Clare, one of the richest women
in England. It is the remains of the 13th-century fortress
that can be seen today atop its 100-foot-high motte.

Clifford Castle, Herefordshire

Clifford, Hereford, HR3 5EU
www.cliffordcastle.org

OWNED BY PAUL RUMPH

The remains of a gatehouse, hall and round towers.
Constructed in 1070 on a cliff overlooking a ford on the
River Wye, the early wooden motte-and-bailey castle was
built to provide protection for a planned Norman
settlement. The stone castle dates from around 1162,
and was the home of Rosamund Clifford, also known as
'Fair Rosamund', mistress of Henry II. During the Owain
Glyndŵr rebellion of 1402, the castle was destroyed by
Welsh forces.

Clitheroe Castle, Lancashire

Castle Hill, Clitheroe, Lancashire, BB7 1BA
01200 424568 | www.lancashire.gov.uk/leisure-and-culture/museums/clitheroe-castle-museum

OWNED BY RIBBLE VALLEY BOROUGH COUNCIL

The remains of a three-storey-high castle keep, with a modern museum. Built in 1186 by Robert de Lacy, the Norman keep of the castle is reputed to be the second smallest in England. The stone keep is enclosed within a curtain wall, only part of which remains. Standing almost three storeys high but now roofless, the keep was damaged by Parliamentary forces during the English Civil War. The castle was privately owned until 1920 when it was sold to the local council to establish a memorial to the First World War. Within the castle grounds is a museum which explains the castle's history.

Clun Castle, Shropshire

Clun, Craven Arms, Shropshire, SY7 8JT
0370 333 1181 | www.english-heritage.org.uk

OWNED BY ENGLISH HERITAGE

Ruins and earthworks of a 13th-century Welsh Border
castle. Built to defend the unsettled border country
between Wales and England shortly after the Norman
Conquest in 1066, the first motte-and-bailey castle at
Clun was constructed of wood. Attacked and burned
down by the Welsh in 1196, it was rebuilt in stone in
the late 13th century by the Fitzallan family. The castle
was converted into a hunting lodge some time in the
14th century, but by the 16th century it was largely
ruined. Today, the remains include the grand four-storey
stone keep and a curtain wall.

Cockermouth Castle, Cumbria

Castlegate, Cockermouth, Cumbria, CA13 9EU

PRIVATELY OWNED BY THE WYNDHAM FAMILY

The ruins of a Norman castle with some Roman stonework visible. Constructed in 1134 using a great deal of stone from a nearby Roman settlement, the castle was enlarged in the 14th century and stands high above the town overlooking the River Derwent. Former owner Pamela Wyndham, Lady Egremont, was a Bletchley Park decoder during the Second World War.

Colchester Castle, Essex

Colchester Castle Museum, Castle Park, Colchester,
Essex, CO1 1TJ
01206 282939 | www.cimuseums.org.uk/visit/venues/
colchester-castle

OWNED BY COLCHESTER & IPSWICH MUSEUM SERVICE

The first of William the Conqueror's great stone keeps
and the largest built by the Normans in Europe. Building
began around 1069 but halted in 1080 due to the threat
of Viking invasion. The castle was completed by 1100
and remains largely intact. Recycled materials from the
former Roman town can clearly be seen in the building
structure. The castle was besieged and eventually captured
by King John in 1215, following his altercation with
rebellious barons. Much of the castle was in ruins by the
16th century, although in 1645 it was serving as the county
prison and Matthew Hopkins, the self-styled Witchfinder
General, interrogated and imprisoned suspected witches
here. In 1922 the castle and parkland were gifted to the
town and it now serves as a public museum.

Conisbrough Castle, South Yorkshire

Castle Hill, Conisbrough, Doncaster, South Yorkshire, DN12 3BU
01709 863329 | www.english-heritage.org.uk

OWNED BY ENGLISH HERITAGE

Set on a natural slope above the Don Valley, Conisbrough Castle is said to have been the inspiration for Sir Walter Scott's novel *Ivanhoe*. Fortified by earthworks, the first castle on the site would have been little more than a wooden palisade, built soon after the Norman Conquest by William of Warenne. Hamelin Plantagenet, King Henry II's half-brother, was responsible for the current stone structure, which features the oldest circular stone keep in England: previously keeps were either square or rectangular in design. The castle gradually fell out of use during the 15th century.

Cooling Castle, Kent

Cooling Road, Rochester, Kent, ME3 8DT

PRIVATELY OWNED

The remains of a 14th-century quadrangular, or courtyard, castle, built by John Cobham in the 1380s to protect the area from French raiders. Despite an unusual layout designed with the use of gunpowder weaponry in mind, the castle was taken by Sir Thomas Wyatt the Younger in less than a day in January 1554 but then allowed to fall into ruin after his defeat by Queen Mary I. During the 17th century a farmhouse, barn and other outhouses were constructed on the site. These buildings saw a number of modifications over the years and are still in use today. The farmhouse is owned by the musician Jools Holland and Cooling Castle Barn is a popular wedding venue.

Corby Castle, Cumbria

Great Corby, Carlisle, Cumbria, CA4 8LR

PRIVATELY OWNED BY EDWARD HAUGHEY
NOT OPEN TO THE PUBLIC

An intact 13th-century pele tower, remodelled in the
early 19th century. Originally built in the 13th century as
a red sandstone pele tower by the Salkeld family, the
fortified tower was sold to Lord William Howard in 1611,
who added a two-storey house. Significant building work
was undertaken for Henry Howard between 1812–17
and the castle remained the ancestral home of the
Howard family until 1994. It is said to be haunted by the
ghost of 'The Radiant Boy'.

Corfe Castle, Wareham, Dorset

The Square, Corfe Castle, Wareham, Dorset, BH20 5EZ
01929 481294 | www.nationaltrust.org.uk/corfe-castle

OWNED BY NATIONAL TRUST

Perched high above Corfe village, the remains of this
early Norman castle cannot fail to impress. Built during
the reign of William the Conqueror, it controls a strategic
passage through the Purbeck Hills. There had been a
fortress on this site long before the Normans arrived,
possibly Roman but certainly Saxon from the 9th century.
In 1635, the castle was sold to Sir John Bankes, who owned
it during the English Civil War. His wife, Lady Mary Bankes,
led the defence of the castle when it was twice besieged
by Parliamentarian troops. The first siege was unsuccessful,
but in 1645 the castle finally succumbed and was
demolished later that year by order of Parliament.

Dalton Castle, Cumbria

Market Place, Dalton-in-Furness, Cumbria, LA15 8AX
01539 560951 | www.nationaltrust.org.uk/dalton-castle

OWNED BY NATIONAL TRUST

There has likely been a defensive structure in Dalton as early as AD 79, but the current castle was built in the early 14th century by the monks of the influential Furness Abbey. This type of structure known as a pele tower was common in northern England, offering protection from raiding Scots. Still standing three storeys high, the castle continued to serve as a courthouse and a prison as border tensions decreased over the centuries. The castle outlived the Abbey, which was disbanded by Henry VIII in 1537.

Dane John Mound, Canterbury, Kent

Castle Row, Watling Street, Canterbury, Kent, CT1 1YW

OWNED BY CANTERBURY CITY COUNCIL

The site of one of the first Norman motte-and-bailey castles to be erected by William the Conqueror following his invasion of 1066. The mound was a former Roman burial site; the Normans simply utilised the existing earthwork to erect their wooden fortification. This early structure was later superseded by the stone fortress of Canterbury Castle, located a short distance away.
The monument was erected in 1803 to commemorate the work of James Simmons who was responsible for landscaping the mound and nearby gardens.

Dartmouth Castle, Devon

Castle Road, Dartmouth, Devon, TQ6 0JN
01803 833588 or 839618 | www.english-heritage.org.uk

OWNED BY ENGLISH HERITAGE

Guarding the narrow entrance to the Dart Estuary and the strategic port of Dartmouth, the castle defences of this fortalice, or coastal fort, were started in 1388 by John Hawley, the enterprising mayor of Dartmouth. Almost a century later the imposing Gun Tower was added, making it the first English coastal fortress specifically built to mount the heavy artillery required to sink shipping. During the Civil War the castle was besieged and subsequently taken by the Royalists, who held it for three years before it was retaken by the Parliamentarians in 1646. The castle battery remained in military use throughout the First and Second World Wars.

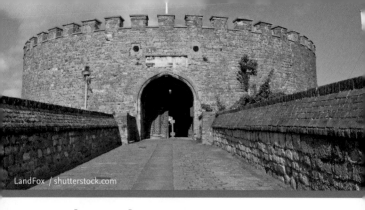
LandFox / shutterstock.com

Deal Castle, Kent

Marine Road, Deal, Kent, CT14 7BA
01304 372762 | www.english-heritage.org.uk

OWNED BY ENGLISH HERITAGE

One of the finest Tudor artillery castles in England. Deal
Castle was built by Henry VIII as part of a line of defences
to protect England's coast from foreign invasion.
Whether by design or coincidence, the Tudor-rose-
shaped fortress was built between 1539–1540 reusing
stone (with a twist of irony) from nearby religious houses
following the Dissolution of the Monasteries.

Deddington Castle, Oxfordshire

Castle Street, Deddington, Oxford, OX15 0TP
0370 333 1181 | www.english-heritage.org.uk

OWNED BY ENGLISH HERITAGE

Extensive earthworks mark the site of this 11th-century Norman motte-and-bailey castle. Built on an earlier Saxon site, the castle was founded by Bishop Odo of Bayeux, half-brother to William the Conqueror. In the late 12th century it was involved in the struggle between King Richard and his brother Prince John, but by the end of the 13th century there appears to have been little of the castle left.

Donnington Castle, West Berkshire

Donnington, West Berkshire, RG14 2LE
0370 333 1181 | www.english-heritage.org.uk

OWNED BY ENGLISH HERITAGE

The remains of a medieval castle and gatehouse. Originally built during the reign of Richard II, all that remains of Donnington Castle today is its gatehouse and scattered earthworks. Before it was demolished in 1646, both King Henry VIII and Queen Elizabeth I visited the castle.

Dover Castle, Kent

Castle Hill, Dover, Kent, CT16 1HU
01304 211 067 | www.english-heritage.org.uk

OWNED BY ENGLISH HERITAGE

Situated above the White Cliffs of Dover, commanding the shortest sea crossing between England and the continent, this grand medieval castle, the largest in England, has a long and fascinating history. Centuries before Henry II founded his great stone castle here in the 1160s the site hosted an Iron Age hill fort, and it still includes a Roman lighthouse. The adjacent Anglo-Saxon church was once part of a Saxon fortified settlement that was converted by William the Conqueror into a Norman earthwork and timber motte-and-bailey castle. In the 13th century King John ordered the construction of underground tunnels to quickly deploy troops in order to surprise attacking forces. These tunnels were later used as a military command HQ during the Second World War.

Dunstanburgh Castle, Craster, Northumberland

Dunstanburgh Road, Craster, Alnwick,
Northumberland, NE66 3TT
01665 576231 | www.english-heritage.org.uk

OWNED BY NATIONAL TRUST

Once one of the largest fortifications in Northern England,
this iconic castle ruin stands on a spectacular headland on
the Northumberland coastline. Although the site shows
evidence of much earlier occupation, the current remains
date from 1313, when Earl Thomas of Lancaster, cousin
of King Edward II, began construction of this massive
fortress. A Lancastrian stronghold during the Wars of the
Roses, the castle suffered major damage and gradually
fell into ruin.

84

Philip Bird LRPS CPAGB / shutterstock.com

Dunster Castle, Somerset

Dunster, near Minehead, Somerset, TA24 6SL
01643 821314 | www.nationaltrust.org.uk/dunster-castle

OWNED BY NATIONAL TRUST

Originally an 11th-century motte-and-bailey timber castle
built by William de Mohun, the castle was expanded with
an additional stone keep in the 12th century, which helped
it to survive attacks in the early years of The Anarchy.
Dunster Castle saw more extensive modernisation and
development via the Luttrell family who resided there
from the 14th century to the 20th century, turning the
castle into the impressive country house we see today.

Durham Castle, County Durham

Palace Green, Durham, DH1 3RW
0191 334 2932 | www.dur.ac.uk/durham.castle

OWNED BY UNIVERSITY OF DURHAM

Built by William the Conqueror in 1072 as part of his
plan to subjugate the northern part of his new kingdom,
Durham Castle is a good example of the early Norman
motte-and-bailey style of fortification. In the Middle
Ages the castle served as a fortress to counter the threat
from the Scots and then became the main residence of
the Prince Bishops of Durham. In 1837, the castle
became part of the new University of Durham and now
serves as a residence for students and dons.

Edlingham Castle,
Northumberland

Edlingham, Alnwick, Northumberland, NE66 2BW
0370 333 1181 | www.english-heritage.org.uk

OWNED BY ENGLISH HERITAGE

The ruins of a 14th-century castle, perhaps more accurately
described as a fortified manor house, with its impressive
leaning tower, it guards the approach to the strategic
stronghold of Alnwick. Its fortifications were increased
in response to the warfare which raged between England
and Scotland in the period between 1300–1600.

Egremont Castle, Cumbria

Bookwell, Egremont, Cumbria, CA22 2JP
www.visitcumbria.com/wc/egremont-castle

DECLARED SCHEDULED ANCIENT MONUMENT

The ruins of a 12th-century castle built on the site of an earlier Danish fort. The present motte-and-bailey castle was built by William de Meschines, first Lord of Egremont, between 1120 and 1135. Extended in the 13th century, when Egremont's renowned annual Crab Fair also began, the castle and its lands passed back and forth between the English and the Scots before finally being destroyed in the 16th century after a failed attempt by local nobles to take the English throne for Mary Queen of Scots. William Wordsworth's 19th-century poem *The Horn of Egremont Castle*, tells the tale of the castle's early owners, the de Lucy family, and their legendary horn, which only the rightful heir could use.

Etal Castle, Northumberland

Cornhill on Tweed, Northumberland, TD12 4TN
01890 820332 | www.english-heritage.org.uk

OWNED BY ENGLISH HERITAGE

Built by Robert Manners in the mid-14th century, these
castle ruins guard a strategic crossing of the River Till.
Primarily constructed as a dwelling house, its location
in the troubled England–Scotland border region meant
that shortly after building it was fortified and strengthened.
The castle fell to James IV's invading Scots army in 1513,
just prior to their crushing defeat at the Battle of Flodden.
The remains of the impressive central keep still stand.

Eynsford Castle, Eynsford, Kent

Eynsford, Kent, DA4 0AA
0370 333 1181 | www.english-heritage.org.uk

OWNED BY ENGLISH HERITAGE

Built around 1088 by William de Eynsford, Sheriff of
Kent, the castle was constructed to an enclosure design,
with an encircling curtain wall protecting the inner
cluster of buildings. The structure differed from other
early Norman castles that followed a motte-and-bailey
plan, which included a central keep. Enlarged a century
later, a great hall and gatehouse were added. Broken
into and ransacked in the 14th century, the castle was
abandoned and fell into ruin.

Farleigh Hungerford Castle, Somerset

Farleigh Hungerford, Norton St Philip, Bath,
Somerset, BA2 7RS
01225 754026 | www.english-heritage.org.uk

OWNED BY ENGLISH HERITAGE

Built by Sir Thomas Hungerford between 1377 and 1383,
Farleigh Hungerford Castle was constructed as a simple
rectangular building with a curtain wall. At the outbreak
of the English Civil War, in 1642, the castle was held by
Sir Edward Hungerford, a leader of Parliamentary forces
in Wiltshire. The castle escaped slighting as a consequence
of this. The last of the Hungerfords to hold the castle,
another Sir Edward, was forced to sell the property in
1686 to settle his gambling debts. By the 18th century
the uninhabited castle had fallen into disrepair.

Farnham Castle Keep, Surrey

Castle Street, Farnham, Surrey, GU9 0AG
01252 721194 | www.english-heritage.org.uk

OWNED BY ENGLISH HERITAGE

The remains of a 12th-century castle. Built by Henry de Blois in 1138, Farnham served as the seat of the powerful Bishops of Winchester for over 800 years. Following The Anarchy, the original motte-and-bailey castle was demolished by Henry II in 1155 and rebuilt again in the late 12th century. In 1648, the castle was slighted again in the aftermath of the English Civil War and the keep was abandoned. However, much-altered parts of the medieval bishops' residence remain.

Fotheringhay Castle, Northamptonshire

Fotheringhay, Northamptonshire, PE8 5HZ

DECLARED SCHEDULED ANCIENT MONUMENT

A motte-and-bailey castle founded in the early 12th century by Simon de Senlis, Earl of Northampton, Fotheringhay Castle was the birthplace of King Richard III in 1452 and later the site of the execution of Mary Queen of Scots in 1587. By the 17th century the castle had been dismantled, leaving only earthworks and some masonry remains from the exterior wall.

Framlingham Castle, Suffolk

Church Street, Framlingham, Suffolk, IP13 9BP
01728 724189 | www.english-heritage.org.uk

OWNED BY ENGLISH HERITAGE

An externally intact, majestic 12th-century fortress. An early
motte-and-bailey Norman castle occupied the site by 1148,
but this was destroyed by King Henry II following the
revolt of 1173–4. Its replacement, built by Roger Bigod
Earl of Norfolk, had no central keep and used a curtain
wall with thirteen strong towers to defend the castle.
Despite these new defences, the castle was taken by
King John in 1216 after a two-day siege. By the end of
the century, Framlingham had become a luxurious
country retreat. The castle was home to Mary Tudor
before she became Queen in 1553.

Goodrich Castle, Ross-on-Wye, Herefordshire

Castle Lane, Goodrich, Ross-on-Wye, Herefordshire, HR9 6HY
01600 890538 | www.english-heritage.org.uk

OWNED BY ENGLISH HERITAGE

The well-preserved ruins of a 13th-century castle, built by Godric of Mappestone following the Norman Conquest of England. Initially a motte-and-bailey fortification, in the middle of the 12th century the original wooden castle was replaced with a stone keep and was then expanded significantly during the late 13th century. Gifted to the famous William Marshal, (the inspiration for the character of William Thatcher played by Heath Ledger in the film *A Knight's Tale*), each of his four sons inherited the castle in turn, the last dying childless in 1245. The site of heavy action during the English Civil War, the castle was bombarded into submission by Parliamentary troops using 'Roaring Meg'. This huge mortar is on display at the castle.

Hadleigh Castle, Essex

Hadleigh, Essex, SS7 2AR
0370 333 1181 | www.english-heritage.org.uk

OWNED BY ENGLISH HERITAGE

The remains of a 13th-century castle. Overlooking the
Thames estuary, the castle was built after 1215 during
the reign of Henry III by Hubert de Burgh. Greatly
expanded by Edward III, the king recognised the strategic
importance of Hadleigh in defending London against
French attacks. Edward also built Queenborough Castle
on the opposite Kent shore. Built on unstable London
clay and subject to subsidence, Hadleigh Castle was
eventually sold for building materials in the 16th century.

Halton Castle, Runcorn

Castle Road, Runcorn, Cheshire, WA7 2BE

OWNED BY THE DUCHY OF LANCASTER

The remains of an 11th-century castle. Once the seat of the Barons of Halton, Halton Castle was badly damaged during the Civil War although parts of the structure such as the gatehouse were in use until 1737. In 1737 a courthouse was built on the site, which also operated as a prison. The courthouse became a public house, still in operation today: the Castle Hotel.

Hastings Castle, East Sussex

Castle Hill Road, Hastings, East Sussex, TN34 3HY
01424 422964 | www.smugglersadventure.co.uk/
hastings-castle-experience

OWNED BY HASTINGS CORPORATION

The first new fortification built by William of Normandy immediately after landing in England in 1066, Hastings was originally a timber and earth motte-and-bailey castle. Built close to the shoreline, William ordered that it should be rebuilt in stone in 1070. King Henry III refortified the castle in 1220, yet less than half a century later violent storms eroded much of the soft sandstone cliffs that the castle had been built upon. Centuries of erosion has seen large sections of the castle lost to the sea.

Hedingham Castle, Essex

Castle Hedingham, Halstead, Essex, CO9 3DJ
01787 460261 | www.hedinghamcastle.co.uk

OWNED BY JASON AND DEMETRA LINDSAY

An intact Norman motte-and-bailey castle and family
home. Built in the late 11th or early 12th century by
Aubrey de Vere, Hedingham Castle was the stronghold
of the de Vere family for 550 years. The castle was
besieged twice, in 1216 and 1217, during the dispute
between King John and the rebel barons. The castle has
had a number of interesting owners since then,
including the Lord Mayor of London Sir William
Ashhurst MP. Fittingly, the current owners are also
descendants of Aubrey de Vere.

Bewickswan / shutterstock.com

Helmsley Castle, Yorkshire

Castlegate, Helmsley, North Yorkshire, YO62 5AB
01439 770442 | www.english-heritage.org.uk

OWNED BY THE FEVERSHAM FAMILY
CARED FOR BY ENGLISH HERITAGE

The remains of a medieval castle. Originally constructed
in wood around 1120 by Walter Espec, who was also
responsible for the founding of nearby Rievaulx Abbey,
the castle was rebuilt in stone by Robert de Roos at the
beginning of the 13th century. Helmsley was again
remodelled into a more comfortable residence by the
Manners family during the 16th century. Besieged by
Parliamentary troops for three months in 1644, the
garrison finally surrendered and it became home to the
Duke of Buckingham and his wife, who was the
daughter of Parliamentary commander, Thomas Fairfax.

Herstmonceux Castle, Hailsham, East Sussex

Herstmonceux Castle, Gardens & Grounds, Wartling Road Entrance, Hailsham, East Sussex, BN27 1RN
www.herstmonceux-castle.com

OWNED BY BADER INTERNATIONAL STUDY CENTRE
NOT OPEN TO THE PUBLIC

An intact brick-built Tudor castle. Built by Sir Roger Fiennes following his appointment as Treasurer to the Household of King Henry VI, construction of this red brick moated castle started in 1441. More of a palatial residence than a defensive structure, it cost £3,000 to build. Sold to George Naylor a London lawyer in 1708, it was Naylor's grandson who reduced the castle to a picturesque ruin by demolishing its interior. Restored in the early 1900s, it is now home to the Bader International Study Centre for Queen's University in Canada.

Hever Castle, Edenbridge, Kent

Hever Castle and Gardens, Hever, Edenbridge, Kent, TN8 7NG
01732 865224 | www.hevercastle.co.uk

OWNED BY BROADLAND PROPERTIES LIMITED

An intact, mainly Tudor castle. It was in the early 1500s that the Bullen family bought the castle and added a Tudor dwelling within its walls, however parts of the castle date back to 1270. The childhood home of its most famous inhabitant, Anne Boleyn, it later passed to Henry VIII's fourth wife, Anne of Cleves. Today the castle offers accommodation, golf, venue hire and a number of public events throughout the year.

Hurst Castle, Lymington, Hampshire

Keyhaven, Lymington, Hampshire, SO41 0TR
01590 642500 | www.hurstcastle.co.uk

OWNED BY ENGLISH HERITAGE
MANAGED BY HURST MARINE

An intact Tudor coastal artillery castle. Built by Henry VIII
as part of a chain of defences to protect England's coast
from foreign invasion. The circular stone tower,
strengthened by semi-circular bastions, was completed
by the end of 1544 to guard the narrow entrance to the
Solent and the approaches to Southampton.

Hylton Castle, Hylton Dene, Northumberland

Craigavon Road, Castletown, Sunderland,
Tyne and Wear, SR5 3PA
0370 333 1181 | www.english-heritage.org.uk

OWNED BY ENGLISH HERITAGE

The remains of the gatehouse tower of a medieval castle
which, is richly decorated with coats of arms and other
heraldic devices. Originally constructed from wood by
the Hylton (Hilton) family shortly after the Norman
Conquest of 1066, this fortified manor house was
rebuilt in stone around 1400. The castle remained the
principal seat of the Hylton family until the death of the
last baron in 1746.

Kendal Castle, Cumbria

Castle Road, Kendal, Lake District, Cumbria, LA9 7AU

MANAGED BY SOUTH LAKELAND DISTRICT COUNCIL

The ruins of an early 13th-century castle. Built around 1200 as the home of the barons of Kendal, the castle later became home to the Parr family. Although the Parrs occupied Kendal for four centuries, the family had long since deserted the castle by the time Catherine Parr, the sixth and last queen of Henry VIII, was born. The building was already a ruin in Tudor times, however some imposing stonework still remains.

Kenilworth Castle, Warwickshire

Castle Green, off Castle Road, Kenilworth,
Warwickshire, CV8 1NG
01926 852078 | www.english-heritage.org.uk

OWNED BY ENGLISH HERITAGE

The ruined remains of a medieval castle / palace fortress.
Perhaps best known as the home of Robert Dudley, the
favourite of Queen Elizabeth I, who in 1575 created this
semi-royal palace in order to impress his queen.
Kenilworth was actually founded around 1120 by
Geoffrey de Clinton, Chamberlain to Henry I, who
constructed the strong central keep. By damming and
diverting local streams, huge water defences were added.
In the centuries that followed, vast sums of money were
spent to transform the medieval castle into a palace
fortress. In 1649, Kenilworth was partly destroyed and
the moat drained by Parliamentary forces to prevent it
being used as a military stronghold again.

Kimbolton Castle, Cambridgeshire

Kimbolton, Huntingdon, Cambridgeshire, PE28 0EA
01480 860505 | www.kimbolton.cambs.sch.uk/castle

OWNED BY KIMBOLTON SCHOOL

A medieval castle converted into an 18th-century palace.
Although parts of the original Tudor manor house can
still be seen, the majority of the castle was built between
1690 and 1720. The most famous resident was Katherine
of Aragon who was detained here after her divorce from
Henry VIII. Today the castle houses Kimbolton School.

Kirby Muxloe Castle, Leicestershire

Off Oakcroft Ave, Kirby Muxloe, Leicestershire, LE9 2DH
01162 386886 | www.english-heritage.org.uk

OWNED BY ENGLISH HERITAGE

This moated 15th-century castle was left unfinished when
its owner was executed for treason. The owner was William,
1st Baron Hastings, who began building the castle in
1480 during the Wars of the Roses. Building work
stopped abruptly in 1483 when William was executed
for treason by Richard III and it was never completed.
Parts of the castle were occupied by remaining members
of the Hastings family but by the 16th century the site
lay in ruin.

Knaresborough Castle, North Yorkshire

Castle Yard, Knaresborough, North Yorkshire, HG5 8AS
01423 556188 | www.harrogate.gov.uk/info/20153/
knaresborough_castle_and_museum

OWNED BY DUCHY OF LANCASTER
ADMINISTERED BY HARROGATE BOROUGH COUNCIL

The remains of a medieval fortress. Strategically placed at the top of a large cliff offering commanding views of the River Nidd, the first castle was erected shortly after the Norman Conquest of England and was later reinforced by King Henry I. Following the murder of Thomas Becket in 1170, Hugh de Moreville and his fellow assassins took refuge in Knaresborough Castle. Viewed as an important northern fortress by English royalty, King John, Edward I and Edward II all lavished funds on strengthening and improving its defences. Like most other castles across the country, Knaresborough met its end following the Civil War when, in 1648, it was blown up, or slighted, on the orders of Parliament to prevent any future use as a military structure.

Lancaster Castle, Lancashire

Lancaster Castle, Castle Parade, Lancaster,
Lancashire, LA1 1YJ
01524 64998 | www.lancastercastle.com

OWNED BY THE DUCHY OF LANCASTER

An intact medieval castle and former prison. Occupying
the site of a former Roman fort at a crossing of the
River Lune, a wooden Saxon fort was demolished in
order to make way for this Norman castle, built around
1088 by Roger de Poitou. In 1322 and again in 1389,
invading Scots attacked and burned Lancaster,
damaging but not taking the castle. The castle did not
see military action again until the English Civil War when
it changed hands several times before being slighted.
Parts of the castle used for the gaol and courts were
spared. The castle is still used as a Crown Court today.

Launceston Castle, Cornwall

Castle Lodge, Launceston, Cornwall, PL15 7DR
01566 772365 | www.english-heritage.org.uk

OWNED BY ENGLISH HERITAGE

The ruins of an early 13th-century castle. Set on a large
natural mound controlling the strategic crossing of the
River Tamar, a wooden motte-and-bailey castle was
erected shortly after the Norman Conquest, possibly as
early as 1067. During the 13th century, Richard Earl of
Cornwall, younger brother of Henry III, began to rebuild
the castle in stone. The castle was used for many years as
an assizes (civil and criminal court) and gaol.

Leeds Castle, Kent

Leeds Castle, Maidstone, Kent, ME17 1RG
01622 765400 | www.leeds-castle.com

OWNED BY LEEDS CASTLE FOUNDATION

One of the most beautiful and intact medieval castles in England, Leeds dates back to 1119 when it was built as a Norman stronghold. However, it was in 1278 that the castle saw significant investment when it became the property of King Edward I. As his favoured residence, Edward greatly enhanced its defences and created the lake that surrounds the castle. Henry VIII was also a great fan of Leeds and made many Tudor additions.

Lewes Castle, East Sussex

Lewes Castle & Museum, 169 High Street, Lewes,
East Sussex, BN7 1YE
01273 486290 | sussexpast.co.uk/properties-to-discover/
lewes-castle

OWNED BY SUSSEX PAST

The remains of a Norman castle. Built by William de
Warenne around 1069, the first fortification on the site
was a wooden keep that was later converted to stone.
Unusually for a Norman motte-and-bailey castle, it was
built with two mottes. Standing at the highest point of
Lewes, the castle comprises a keep with octagonal towers
and a particularly fine example of a 14th-century barbican,
a defensive tower gateway. A museum in Barbican House
relates the history of the castle and town.

Lincoln Castle, Lincolnshire

Castle Square, Lincoln, Lincolnshire, LN1 3AA
01522 554559 | www.lincolncastle.com

OWNED BY LINCOLNSHIRE COUNTY COUNCIL

One of the more well-preserved castles in England.
Constructed by order of William the Conqueror on the
site of a pre-existing Roman fortress, the castle was started
in 1068, just two years after the Norman Conquest.
One of the first structures on the site was the Lucy Tower
motte-and-bailey, to which another motte and stone
walls were added early in the 12th century. The outer
bailey stretched around the entire medieval city of
Lincoln. For 900 years it operated as a court and prison,
its early prisoners suffering execution on the castle
ramparts. Still home to the Crown Courts, the castle is
open to the public as a museum and displays an original
copy of the Magna Carta.

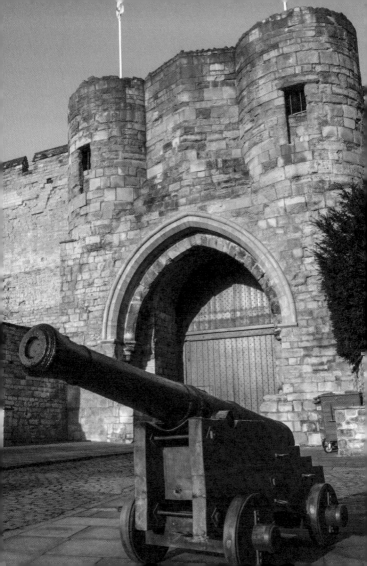

Lindisfarne Castle, Holy Island, Northumberland

Holy Island, Berwick-upon-Tweed, Northumberland, TD15 2SH
01289 389244 | www.nationaltrust.org.uk/lindisfarne-castle

OWNED BY NATIONAL TRUST

A Tudor fort, converted into an Edwardian holiday home. Fearing a possible Scottish invasion, Henry VIII ordered defences to be built in 1542. The site of the castle on Beblowe Crag was first fortified in 1547. Between 1570 and 1571, Elizabeth I updated and strengthened the defences by adding new gun platforms. The need for a castle declined when, in 1603, James VI and I came to power and combined the Scottish and English thrones. Accordingly the garrison continued to shrink over the next few hundred years. The castle was converted into a holiday home in 1903 by Arts and Crafts architect Edward Lutyens for his friend Edward Hudson, the proprietor of *Country Life* magazine.

Ludgershall Castle, Wiltshire

Castle Street, Ludgershall, Wiltshire, SP11 9QT
0370 333 1181 | www.english-heritage.org.uk

OWNED BY ENGLISH HERITAGE

The remains of a 12th century fortified royal residence.
Just 10 miles from prehistoric Stonehenge, this medieval
fortress was built in the late 11th century by Edward of
Salisbury, Sheriff of Wiltshire. Set within two adjacent
enclosures, the castle is surrounded by earthwork banks
and ditches. In 1210 King John strengthened the castle
and improved the living quarters. John's son, Henry III,
completed the transformation into a comfortable royal
residence and hunting lodge. The castle gradually fell
out of use and by 1540 many of the buildings had been
pulled down, with the crumbling tower retained as a
garden feature.

Ludlow Castle, Shropshire

Castle Square, Ludlow, Shropshire, SY8 1AY
01584 874465 | www.ludlowcastle.com

OWNED BY THE HERBERT FAMILY

Originally constructed to control the troubled Welsh
Borders, the first fortress at Ludlow was built shortly after
the Norman Conquest. Passing down through generations
of the influential de Lacy family, it was transformed into
a magnificent palace for Roger Mortimer, then the most
powerful man in England. Ludlow became Crown property
in 1461, and under the ownership of Richard Plantagenet,
Duke of York, it became a major base in the Wars of the
Roses. It later became a royal palace and brief home to
the 'Princes in the Tower' before they were taken to the
Tower of London. In 1669 when the seat of
administration for Wales and the Marches moved to
London, the castle was abandoned and fell into ruin.

129

Lydford Castle, near Okehampton, Devon

Lydford, Okehampton, Devon, EX20 4BH
0370 333 1181 | www.english-heritage.org.uk

OWNED BY ENGLISH HERITAGE

The remains of a 13th-century square tower keep.
The original medieval castle was actually a courtroom
and prison built about 1195, which took the form of a
freestanding tower at least two storeys high. The castle
was rebuilt in the 13th century by digging a ditch around
the tower and piling up the soil to the level of the
ground floor. The upper storeys were completely rebuilt
to form a small keep and the interior of the old prison
was filled in. Mention must also be made of the Saxon
town defences to the north of the village.

Maiden Castle, Dorset

Winterborne Monkton, Dorchester, Dorset, DT2 9EY
0370 333 1181 | www.english-heritage.org.uk

OWNED BY ENGLISH HERITAGE

Maiden Castle is the largest Iron Age hill fort in Europe and covers an area of 47 acres. 'Maiden' derives from the Celtic 'Mai Dun' which means 'great hill'. It is situated just 2 miles south of Dorchester in Dorset. It is thought that the construction of Maiden Castle began around 3000 BC. The present hill fort as we see it today, was started during the Iron Age around 450–300 BC and was held by Iron Age tribes until the Roman invasion in AD 43. A Roman temple was built at Maiden Castle in the 4th century, the foundations of which can still be seen today. The fort was abandoned shortly after this time, although it may have been occupied during early Saxon times. It has certainly been deserted for the last 1400 years or so.

Middleham Castle, North Yorkshire

Castle Hill, Middleham, North Yorkshire, DL8 4QG
0196 962 3899 | www.english-heritage.org.uk

OWNED BY ENGLISH HERITAGE

The extensive remains of a medieval fortified palace. Built by Robert Fitzrandolph around 1190, this early motte-and-bailey castle came into the hands of the powerful Neville family in 1270. Following the Battle of Barnet in 1471 it was seized by the Crown. The childhood home of King Richard III, the castle remained in royal hands until the reign of James VI and I when it was sold. The castle was finally slighted during the English Civil War. Only the keep and castle walls survive as testament to the might of this imposing royal fortress.

Mitford Castle, Northumberland

Mitford, Morpeth, Northumberland, NE61 3PY

OWNED BY THE BRUCE SHEPHERD FAMILY

The 11th-century Mitford Castle was originally home to the Mitford family, whose descendants include the famous 20th century 'Mitford sisters'. Following the Norman Conquest, the castle was gifted to the Norman knight Richard Bertram by William the Conqueror. Over the next few hundred years, the castle changed hands between the English and the Scots. In the early 14th century, when it had been commandeered by the notorious kidnapper Sir Gilbert de Middleton, the castle was badly damaged and never rebuilt. Stones from the ruins were removed for other structures, including the nearby manor house, which became the second seat of the Mitford family in the 16th century. The Mitford estate, including the castle, was sold in 1993 to the Bruce Shepherd family who are working with English Heritage to restore and preserve the site.

Muncaster Castle, Ravenglass, Cumbria

Ravenglass, Cumbria, CA18 1RQ
01229 717 614 | www.muncaster.co.uk

OWNED BY THE PENNINGTON FAMILY

An intact medieval castle, now home to the Pennington
family. The oldest part of the castle is the pele tower,
which dates from the early 1300s. Pele towers were
fortified homes, built as a refuge from attack, commonly
found along the troubled border region between
England and Scotland. The tower was gradually added to
and altered over the years, becoming the comfortable
family home that it is now. The castle's tapestry room is
reputed to be haunted by a wicked jester.

Phillip Maguire / shutterstock.com

Naworth Castle, Cumbria

Brampton, Cumbria, CA8 2HF
016977 3229 | www.naworth.co.uk

OWNED BY THE HOWARD FAMILY
NOT OPEN TO THE PUBLIC

An intact medieval castle. Also known as Naward, the castle
was the seat of the Barons Dacre, now Earls of Carlisle.
Dating from the 13th century, the fortified castle has
been transformed and adapted over centuries to
residential use.

Newark Castle, Nottinghamshire

Newark Castle and Gardens, Castlegate, Newark,
Nottinghamshire, NG24 1BG
01636 650000 | www.newark-sherwooddc.gov.uk/
newarkcastle

OWNED BY NEWARK CORPORATION

The remains of a medieval royal castle. Founded in the
mid-12th century by Alexander, Bishop of Lincoln,
the original timber castle was rebuilt in stone towards
the end of the century. The castle belonged to King John,
and it was here that he died in 1216 following his
infamous 'surfeit of peaches'. Following the English Civil
War, the castle was slighted and left derelict.
Some restoration of the buildings began in the 1840s.

Newcastle Castle Keep, Tyne & Wear

Newcastle Castle, The Black Gate, Castle Garth,
Newcastle upon Tyne, Tyne and Wear, NE1 1RQ
0191 230 6300 | www.newcastlecastle.co.uk

OWNED BY NEWCASTLE CITY COUNCIL

On a site occupied since Roman times, an earth and
timber motte-and-bailey castle was erected in 1080 by
Robert Curthose, eldest son of William the Conqueror.
Built to defend his new kingdom from the Scots, this
'New Castle upon Tyne' guarded a strategic crossing of
the river. Rebuilt in stone by King Henry II around 1175,
the Black Gate was added by Henry III between 1247 and
1250. Refortified in 1643 during the English Civil War,
the castle's 1,500 strong Royalist garrison was besieged
for three months before finally surrendering to a
Scottish army comprising 40,000 troops, under the
command of General Leslie, Lord Leven.

Norham Castle, Northumberland

Castle Street, Norham, Northumberland, TD15 2JY
0370 333 1181 | www.english-heritage.org.uk

OWNED BY ENGLISH HERITAGE

A partly ruined, medieval border castle. Commanding a
vital ford over the River Tweed, the castle was founded by
Ranulf Flambard, Bishop of Durham, who gave orders
for its construction in 1121 to protect his property from
Scottish raids. In the centuries that followed, Norham
was transformed into one of the most powerful border
castles. It was besieged at least 13 times, once for nearly
a year by Robert Bruce. It withstood all that was thrown
against it except the last raid; in 1513 King James IV of
Scotland battered the castle into submission using heavy
cannon, shortly before his defeat at Flodden.

Norwich Castle, Norfolk

Norwich Castle Museum and Art Gallery, Castle Hill,
Norwich, NR1 3JU
01603 493625 / 495897 | www.museums.norfolk.gov.uk/
norwich-castle

OWNED BY CITY OF NORWICH

An intact Norman castle keep, now a museum. Intent on
subjugating East Anglia, William the Conqueror ordered
the first motte-and-bailey castle to be built in 1067.
The stone keep, which still stands today, was built some
60 years later. Serving as a gaol between 1220 and 1887,
the castle was bought by the city of Norwich to be used
as a museum.

Nunney Castle, Somerset

Castle Street, Nunney, near Frome, Somerset, BA11 4LW
0370 333 1181 | www.english-heritage.org.uk

OWNED BY ENGLISH HERITAGE

A moated castle built in the late 14th century by Sir John
Delamare, using the fortune he made as a soldier fighting
in the Hundred Years War with France. Ironically, the
architectural style that he adopted for Nunney appears
to have been borrowed from the French castles he had
undoubtedly besieged and destroyed! Damaged by
cannon fire during the English Civil War the castle fell
into ruins, although it is still considered to be one of the
most impressive castles in Somerset.

Okehampton Castle, Devon

Castle Lodge, Okehampton, Devon, EX20 1JA
01837 52844 | www.english-heritage.org.uk

OWNED BY ENGLISH HERITAGE

The remains of the largest medieval castle in Devon,
Okehampton was built by Baldwin FitzGilbert shortly
after the Norman Conquest of England. This early
motte-and-bailey type fortification was constructed to
control strategic crossings and approaches; the castle
guards a crossing point across the West Okement River.
The castle was used as a fortification until the late
13th century when its owners, the de Courtenays,
became the Earls of Devon and redeveloped the castle as
a luxurious hunting lodge. Although heavily involved in
the 15th-century Wars of the Roses, the castle remained
in good condition until Henry VIII executed Henry
Courtenay in 1538. Thereafter it was abandoned and
gradually fell into ruin, although the central keep still sits
proudly atop its motte.

Old Sarum, Wiltshire

Castle Road, Salisbury, Wiltshire, SP1 3SD
01722 335398 | www.english-heritage.org.uk

OWNED BY ENGLISH HERITAGE

Old Sarum was originally a huge, oval-shaped Iron Age
hill fort protected by equally massive banks and ditches.
Later occupied by the Romans, it became the town of
Sorviodunum. The Saxons then used the site for protection
against Viking raiders, and the Normans added a stone
curtain wall and built a castle above. King Henry I added
a royal palace and a Norman cathedral was constructed
toward the western end of the mound. In 1219, the
cathedral was demolished in favour of a new one built
closer to the river, then called New Salisbury or New
Sarum. The castle fell out of use some years later and
was sold for building materials by Henry VIII.

Old Wardour Castle, Tisbury, Wiltshire

Near Tisbury, Salisbury, Wiltshire, SP3 6RR
01747 870487 | www.english-heritage.org.uk

OWNED BY ENGLISH HERITAGE

Built in the 14th century by John Lord Lovel as a lightly fortified luxury residence with lavish entertainment in mind. The castle comprises a five-sided tower around a central courtyard and in its day was one of the grandest, most innovative homes in England. The castle was later remodelled as an Elizabethan manor by the Arundell family. Wardour suffered badly during the English Civil War, blown up by both sides. The Arundell family ended up building New Wardour Castle to replace it in 1776. The remains of the Old Castle were integrated into the surrounding parkland as a romantic ruin feature.

Orford Castle, Suffolk

Orford, Woodbridge, Suffolk, IP12 2ND
01394 450472 | www.english-heritage.org.uk

OWNED BY ENGLISH HERITAGE

A well-preserved Norman keep. With views over Orford
Ness, the castle was built between 1165 and 1173 by
King Henry II to consolidate royal power in the region
and to act as a coastal defence at a time when powerful
nobles were challenging the authority of the crown.
Orford is built to a keep-and-bailey plan, with a strong
central keep surrounded by a curtain wall. The outer curtain
wall has all but disappeared, however the central tower
keep is very much intact and stands tall beside the pretty
town and former port also developed here by Henry II.

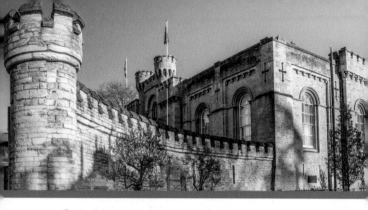

Oxford Castle, Oxfordshire

44–46 Oxford Castle, Oxford, OX1 1AY
01865 260666 | www.oxfordcastleunlocked.co.uk

OWNED BY OXFORDSHIRE COUNTY COUNCIL

A large, partly ruined Norman medieval castle. Built by
Robert d'Oilly in 1071, the original wooden motte-and-
bailey castle was rebuilt in stone during the 11th century.
During The Anarchy in 1147, Matilda occupied the castle
against the forces of her cousin, King Stephen. Matilda
escaped by being lowered from the tower and fleeing
across the frozen Thames. Much of the castle was
destroyed by Parliamentary forces during the English
Civil War, with the remaining buildings used as Oxford's
local gaol. The medieval remains of the castle, including
the motte and St George's Tower, have been preserved.

Pendennis Castle, Falmouth, Cornwall

Falmouth, Cornwall, TR11 4LP
01326 316594 | www.english-heritage.org.uk

OWNED BY ENGLISH HERITAGE

An intact Tudor artillery castle, built by Henry VIII to protect England's coast from potential foreign invasion. The circular stone tower enclosed by a lower curtain wall was completed in 1539 to guard the entrance to the River Fal. In 1646 during the English Civil War, the castle withstood a five-month siege before finally surrendering to Parliamentary forces, the last Royalist position in the west of England to fall.

Pendragon Castle, Outhgill, Cumbria

B6259, Kirkby Stephen, Cumbria, CA17 4JT

DECLARED SCHEDULED ANCIENT MONUMENT

The ruins of a 12th-century castle. According to local legend, the castle was built by Uther Pendragon, father of King Arthur, although there appears to be no evidence of any pre-Norman use of the site. Indeed, the castle was built in the 12th century by Ranulph de Meschines as a fortified pele or tower house. Later it passed into the ownership of Sir Hugh de Morville, one of the four knights who murdered Thomas Becket in 1170. The castle was attacked by Scottish raiding parties on at least two occasions between 1342 and 1541, the latter raid rendering it uninhabitable. Rebuilt in 1660 by Lady Anne Clifford, it quickly fell back into ruin after she died.

Penrith Castle, Cumbria

Castle Terrace, Penrith, Cumbria, CA11 7EA
0370 333 1181 | www.english-heritage.org.uk

OWNED BY ENGLISH HERITAGE

The ruins of a 14th-century sandstone castle. The oldest
part of the castle is the pele tower, which dates from the
late 1300s. Pele towers were fortified homes, built as a
refuge from attack, commonly found along the troubled
border region between England and Scotland. The castle
was subsequently strengthened and transformed into a
luxurious residence by Richard, Duke of Gloucester
(later Richard III). However by the late 1500s, the castle
was in a sad state of repair and was dismantled after
the English Civil War.

Pevensey Castle, East Sussex

Castle Road, Pevensey, East Sussex, BN24 5LE
01323 762604 | www.english-heritage.org.uk

OWNED BY ENGLISH HERITAGE

The substantial remains of a 3rd-century Roman and 11th-century Norman fortress. The Roman fort of Anderitum was built during the 3rd century to protect the southern coastline of Britain from Saxon raiders. It was a descendant of those Saxon raiders, Harold Godwinson (King Harold II) who waited in the fort with his English army for the impending invasion of Duke William of Normandy in the summer of 1066. Shortly after the Conquest a full-scale Norman castle, with a great square keep and a powerful gatehouse, was built within the Roman fort. The castle was besieged in the Rebellion of 1088 and and once again during a period of civil war known as The Anarchy. It remained in use throughout the Late Middle Ages, before falling into disrepair in the centuries that followed.

Peveril Castle, Castleton, Derbyshire

Market Place, Castleton, Derbyshire, S33 8WQ
01433 620613 | www.english-heritage.org.uk

OWNED BY ENGLISH HERITAGE

A ruined, late medieval castle. Set high on a hill above the village of Castleton this stronghold, formerly known as Peak Castle, was built by William Peveril around 1080, shortly after the Norman Conquest of England. The original wooden fortress was soon rebuilt in stone and in 1157 was the venue for a meeting between Henry I and King Malcolm of Scotland. The castle gradually fell into disuse after the 14th century.

Pickering Castle, North Yorkshire

Castlegate, Pickering, North Yorkshire, YO18 7AX
01751 474989 | www.english-heritage.org.uk

OWNED BY ENGLISH HERITAGE

First constructed as a Norman timber and earth motte-
and-bailey castle around 1070, the castle was rebuilt in
stone between 1180 and 1187, with later fortifications
added in the 11th and 12th centuries. The castle remains
are particularly well-preserved as it was one of only a
few fortifications largely unaffected by the 15th-century
Wars of the Roses and the English Civil War of the
17th century.

Piel Castle, Barrow-in-Furness, Cumbria

Piel Island, Barrow-in-Furness, Cumbria, LA13 0QN
0370 333 1181 | www.english-heritage.org.uk

OWNED BY ENGLISH HERITAGE

The ruins of a 14th-century castle. Replacing an earlier
wooden tower, the Abbot of Furness constructed his stone
motte-and-bailey castle on the south-eastern point of
Piel Island around 1327, to guard the deep-water harbour
of Barrow-in-Furness against pirates and Scottish
raiders. The castle also allowed the monks to monitor
the traffic passing through Piel Harbour on its way to
their holdings in Ireland and the Isle of Man. In 1537,
when Furness Abbey was dissolved, the castle became
the property of Henry VIII and was left to fall into ruins.

Pontefract Castle, West Yorkshire

Pontefract Castle, Castle Garth, Pontefract,
West Yorkshire, WF8 1QH
01977 723440 | www.pontefractcastle.co.uk

OWNED BY WAKEFIELD COUNCIL

The remains of a medieval fortress. First constructed as
a Norman timber and earth motte-and-bailey castle by
Ilbert de Lacy around 1070, the castle was rebuilt in stone
shortly afterwards. In the 12th century, the de Lacy family
failed to support King Henry I during his power struggle
with brother Robert and as a result the castle passed to
the Crown. Pontefract is best known as the place where
Richard II died, probably murdered, in 1399. One of the
most important fortresses in the north, the castle housed
a Royalist garrison in the English Civil War and was
eventually destroyed by Parliamentarians after 1649.

Portchester Castle, Portsmouth, Hampshire

Church Road, Portchester, Hampshire, PO16 9QW
02392 378291 | www.english-heritage.org.uk

OWNED BY ENGLISH HERITAGE

The best-preserved of the Roman 'Saxon Shore' forts. The original Roman fort was built between AD 285 and AD 290 to protect the southern coastline of Britain from Saxon raiders. Possibly home to the Roman fleet that defended Britain, when the fort was abandoned it eventually found use as a high-status Saxon residence. In the medieval period, King Henry I added to the defences and Richard II built a series of domestic quarters, including a great hall and kitchens. The castle passed out of royal control in 1632 when Charles I sold it, and was last used during the Napoleonic Wars (1803–1815) as a gaol for over 7,000 French prisoners.

Portland Castle, Weymouth, Dorset

Liberty Road, Castletown, Dorset, DT5 1AZ
01305 820539 | www.english-heritage.org.uk

OWNED BY ENGLISH HERITAGE

An intact Tudor coastal artillery castle, built by Henry VIII as part of a chain of defences to protect England's coast in the event of foreign invasion. The low-profile fortress, built of white Portland stone, was completed in 1539 to guard Portland and Weymouth Harbour. The castle experienced its only real action during the English Civil War of 1642–1649. As a Royalist stronghold it was captured and recaptured several times.

Powderham Castle, Devon

Powderham Castle, Kenton, Exeter, Devon, EX6 8JQ
01626 890243 | www.powderham.co.uk

OWNED BY CHARLES COURTENAY, 19TH EARL OF DEVON

A fortified manor house built in the late 14th century
and early 15th century. There has been a manor on the
site since the 11th century but the castle we see today is
the work of Sir Philip Courtenay, son of the first
Courtenay Earl of Devon to own the castle, who began
renovations in 1391. Powderham Castle was badly
damaged during the Civil War although it was repaired
in the early 18th century by Sir William Courtenay.
Further additions to the castle were made in the 18th
and 19th centuries, and in 1952 it was classified as a
Grade I listed building. The castle remains in the
Courtenay family.

Prudhoe Castle, Northumberland

Castle View, Prudhoe, Northumberland, NE42 6NA
01661 833459 | www.english-heritage.org.uk

OWNED BY ENGLISH HERITAGE

Constructed shortly after the Norman Conquest of
England, the original motte-and-bailey fortification was
created some time in the mid-11th century, to guard a
ford across the River Tyne. It was later rebuilt and
strengthened using local stone with a curtain wall and
gatehouse added. In 1173 and again in 1174, William
the Lion of Scotland invaded to claim the earldom of
Northumberland; on both occasions the castle withstood
his attacks. Unlike many similar medieval castles which
fell into ruin when their defensive use faded, Prudhoe
was continuously occupied and in the early 19th-century
a manor house was built within the castle walls. This now
houses a gift shop.

170

Raby Castle, Darlington, County Durham

Raby Castle, Staindrop, Darlington, Co. Durham, DL2 3AH
01833 660202 | www.rabycastle.com

OWNED BY JOHN VANE, LORD BARNARD

An intact 14th-century castle, home of the Vane family. Built by the powerful Neville family in the 14th century, this imposing fortress comprised a curtain wall with eight substantial towers surrounding a central keep, all accessed by a narrow path over the moat. Raby remained in the Neville family until 1569 when, following the failure of the Rising of the North, the castle and its lands were forfeited to the Crown. In 1626, Sir Henry Vane the Elder, Treasurer to Charles I, purchased Raby and the castle has remained home to the Vane family ever since.

Restormel Castle, Lostwithiel, Cornwall

Near Restormel Road, Lostwithiel, Cornwall, PL22 0EE
01208 872687 | www.english-heritage.org.uk

OWNED BY ENGLISH HERITAGE

The well preserved remains of a 13th-century circular
shell keep. Built shortly after the Norman Conquest of
England, initially this early motte-and-bailey type
fortification included an earthen mound topped by a
wooden palisade. Constructed to control strategic
crossings and approaches, the castle overlooks the River
Fowey. Later rebuilt in stone, Restormel is unusual in
that it has a perfectly circular shell keep. Once a
luxurious residence of the Earl of Cornwall, it became
ruined in the years after the English Civil War.

Richmond Castle, North Yorkshire

Tower Street, Richmond, North Yorkshire, DL10 4QW
01748 822493 | www.english-heritage.org.uk

OWNED BY ENGLISH HERITAGE

The extensive remains of a great Norman fortress.
Built shortly after the Norman Conquest, the original
castle was started around 1071. Built to control
strategic crossings and approaches, the castle
commands extensive views over the Yorkshire Dales
and the River Swale. Originally built to subdue the
unruly Saxon North of England, it was rebuilt and
strengthened over the century that followed using
honey-coloured sandstone and grew to become one of
the greatest Norman fortresses in Britain. As a castle
however, Richmond had fallen out of use by the end of
the 14th century.

Rochester Castle, Rochester, Kent

Rochester Castle, Rochester, Kent, ME1 1SW
01634 335882 | www.english-heritage.org.uk

OWNED BY ENGLISH HERITAGE

One of the best-preserved Norman keeps in England.
Strategically placed alongside the London Road and
guarding an important crossing of the River Medway,
this imposing Norman castle was built on the site of an
earlier Roman fort. Using local Kentish ragstone, the
towerkeep was built around 1127 by William of Corbeil,
Archbishop of Canterbury, and still stands 113 feet high.
Held by rebel barons, the castle endured an epic siege
by King John in 1215. John's engineers used the fat of
40 pigs to fire a mine under the keep, bringing a corner
crashing down. The desperate defenders held on for
another two months before being starved out. Rebuilt
under Henry III and Edward I, the castle remained a
viable fortress until the 16th century.

Rufus Castle, Portland, Dorset

Rufus Castle, Portland, Dorset, DT5 1JA

PRIVATELY OWNED

The remains of a 15th-century castle with Norman keep, also known as a 'Bow and Arrow Castle' due to the many medieval gun ports, which are sometimes mistaken for arrow loops. Built on a rocky promontory on the Isle of Portland, it is possible that the first castle on this site was built for William II. In 1142 during the civil war known as The Anarchy, Robert Earl of Gloucester captured the castle from King Stephen on behalf of Empress Matilda. Much of what we see today dates back to the 15th century when the castle was rebuilt by Richard, Duke of York.

Rye Castle, East Sussex

Rye Castle Museum, 3 East Street, Rye, East Sussex,
TN31 7JY
01797 226728 | www.ryemuseum.co.uk

OWNED BY RYE HERITAGE ASSOCIATION

Built around 1249 during the reign of King Henry III,
Rye Castle formed part of his defences against frequent
attacks from the warring French. As one of England's five
historic Cinque Ports, the town of Rye has traditionally
provided one of the main coastal defences for the realm
in exchange for certain trading privileges. The Ypres Tower
was built in the early 14th century to provide such support.
Although the sea has long since retreated, Rye was once
one of the largest and most important harbours in the
country. Ypres Tower now houses one of the two sites of
Rye Castle Museum.

St Briavels Castle, Gloucestershire

Church Street, St Briavels, Lydney, Gloucestershire, GL15 6TA
01594 530272 | www.english-heritage.org.uk

OWNED BY ENGLISH HERITAGE

The remains of a medieval castle. Built by William FitzBaderon around 1086, the original earth and wooden motte-and-bailey fortress was replaced by a 100-foot-tall stone keep some time in the late 12th century. Throughout the medieval period St Briavel's served as a royal administrative centre for the Forest of Dean. Further extended and strengthened during the 13th century, the castle became a favourite hunting lodge of King John. The castle appears to have fallen from royal favour in the centuries that followed and by 1775 was being used as a debtors' prison. Transformed in the 20th century, it was turned into a Youth Hostel.

St Catherine's Castle, Fowey, Cornwall

St Catherine's Cove, Fowey, Cornwall, PL23 1JH
0370 333 1181 | www.english-heritage.org.uk

OWNED BY ENGLISH HERITAGE

Built by Henry VIII to protect England's coast from foreign invasion, this small two-storey Device fort was completed in 1540 to guard Fowey Harbour, an important centre of trade. The 'Devise forts' (or Henrician castles as they were also known) were a series of castles spanning the English and Welsh Coasts and were named after the King's official command for the building work to begin, known as a "*device*" order. Construction of the device forts took nearly 10 years and was vastly expensive, funded in part by the Crown's acquisitions after the dissolution of the monasteries. St Catherine's Castle was later garrisoned by Royalist troops during the first part of the English Civil War (1642-6) and it remained in use as a battery funded by the local townspeople until the end of the Napoleonic Wars in 1815. Following the outbreak of the Crimean War in 1853 the Castle was reopened and extensively redeveloped before being all but abandoned again by the end of the 19th century.

St Mawes Castle, Cornwall

Castle Drive, St Mawes, near Truro, Cornwall, TR2 5DE
01326 270526 | www.english-heritage.org.uk

OWNED BY ENGLISH HERITAGE

A well-preserved Tudor coastal artillery fortress. Built by Henry VIII as part of a chain of defences to protect England's coast from foreign invasion. The clover leaf design of St Mawes represented the most advanced military architecture of the time. Built between 1539 and 1545, it guarded the important anchorage of Carrick Roads. Not designed for defense against a land attack, it was easily taken in 1646 by Parliamentary forces during the English Civil War.

St Michael's Mount, Cornwall

St Michael's Mount, Marazion, Cornwall, TR17 OHS
01736 710265 | www.stmichaelsmount.co.uk

OWNED BY NATIONAL TRUST

The site of a monastery between the 8th and early 11th centuries, the island became a destination for pilgrims. Following the Norman Conquest, the abbey was granted to the Benedictine monks of Mont Saint-Michel in France, who built the church on the island's summit. In 1473, during the War of the Roses, the Earl of Oxford held the island under siege for 23 weeks. During the English Civil War, Royalists held the Mount against the Parliamentary forces of Oliver Cromwell. The island can be visited by boat, or at low tide via a long causeway from the mainland.

Sandal Castle, Wakefield, West Yorkshire

Manygates Lane, Wakefield, West Yorkshire, WF2 7DS
01977 722741 | www.wakefield.gov.uk

OWNED BY WAKEFIELD COUNCIL

Built shortly after the Norman Conquest to control strategic crossings and approaches, Sandal Castle has extensive views over the River Calder. It was originally built to subdue the rebellious Saxon North of England, it was then rebuilt and strengthened during the 13th century using local stone. The castle is best known for the famous Battle of Wakefield, which was fought nearby during the Wars of the Roses in 1460. Richard, Duke of York, was killed in the battle. During the English Civil War of the 1640s the castle was besieged twice by Parliamentary forces and later stripped of its defences.

Scarborough Castle,
North Yorkshire

Castle Road, Scarborough, North Yorkshire, YO11 1HY
01723 372451 | www.english-heritage.org.uk

OWNED BY ENGLISH HERITAGE

The remains of a medieval Royal fortress. On a site
previously fortified by the Romans, Saxons and Vikings,
the original Norman wooden castle was built in the 1130s
and strengthened from 1150 onwards using local stone.
Over the centuries, structures were added and reinforced,
with medieval monarchs in particular investing heavily in
its upkeep to guard the Yorkshire coastline from the
threat of Scottish and overseas invasion. Peace with
Scotland and the end of the continental wars led to the
decline of the fortress in the 17th century. Scarborough
Castle has been a ruin since the sieges of the English
Civil War, between 1642 and 1648.

Scotney Castle, Tunbridge Wells, Kent

Lamberhurst, Tunbridge Wells, Kent, TN3 8JN
01892 893820 | www.nationaltrust.org.uk/
scotney-castle

OWNED BY NATIONAL TRUST

The ruins of a 14th-century moated castle. Construction of the castle began around 1380. Originally built as a fortified house with towers in each corner, it was rebuilt in Elizabethan style in 1580 and again in 1630. The Catholic Darrell family, who owned the estate for some 350 years, hid Jesuit priests who were preaching at a time when Catholicism was illegal in England. When the new country house was built in 1843 the old castle was left ruined as a romantic garden feature.

Sherborne Old Castle, Dorset

Castleton, Sherborne, Dorset, DT9 3SA
01935 812730 | www.english-heritage.org.uk

OWNED BY ENGLISH HERITAGE

A ruined 12th-century castle that survives within the grounds of a Tudor mansion. The original castle was built as the fortified palace of Roger de Caen, Bishop of Salisbury. During the English Civil War, Sherborne was a Royalist stronghold. Following an eleven day siege in 1645 the old castle was left in ruins by Parliamentary forces under the command of General Fairfax.

Shrewsbury Castle, Shropshire

Castle Street, Shrewsbury, Shropshire, SY1 2AT
01743 358516 | www.shrewsburymuseum.org.uk/
visit-shrewsbury/shrewsbury-castle

OWNED BY SHROPSHIRE COUNCIL

The oldest parts of Shrewsbury Castle were built by the
1st Earl of Shrewsbury, Roger de Montgomery, shortly
after the Norman Conquest. In 1215, the Welsh Prince
Llewelyn seized both the town and castle, and later it was
held by enemies of Edward III during the Barons' War.
Around 1300, during his conflicts with the Welsh,
Edward I greatly enlarged the castle, but it gradually fell
into disuse following his invasion of Wales. In the 18th
century the eminent engineer Thomas Telford remodelled
the castle interiors to serve as a private house. In 1924 it
was acquired by the Corporation of Shrewsbury.

Skipton Castle, North Yorkshire

Skipton, North Yorkshire, BD23 1AW
01756 792442 | www.skiptoncastle.co.uk

OWNED BY THE FATTORINI FAMILY

One of the most complete medieval castles in England.
The original earth and wood motte-and-bailey fortification
built in 1090 by Robert de Romille was rebuilt in stone
shortly afterwards to withstand attacks from raiding Scots.
In 1310, Edward II granted the castle to Robert Clifford
who ordered many improvements to the fortifications.
During the English Civil War the castle was a Royalist
stronghold. Following a three-year siege in 1645 it
surrendered to Oliver Cromwell's Parliamentarians.
After the siege, Lady Anne Clifford ordered the necessary
repairs to the castle. Local legend has it that during the
siege the castle walls were draped with sheep fleeces to
deaden the impact of incoming cannon fire.

Spofforth Castle, North Yorkshire

Castle Street, Spofforth, North Yorkshire, HG3 1ND
0370 333 1181 | www.english-heritage.org.uk

OWNED BY ENGLISH HERITAGE

Built by Henry de Percy in the early 14th-century,
Spofforth Castle was further expanded in the 14th and
15th centuries to the layout that exists today. The castle
was damaged by the Yorkists during the Wars of the Roses
and lay in ruins for almost 100 years until it was later
rebuilt by Henry, Lord Percy in 1559. Suffering further
damage during the English Civil War of 1642–46, it lapsed
into ruin. Today the site is a Grade II listed building.

Sutton Valence Castle, Kent

Rectory Lane, Sutton Valence, Maidstone, Kent, ME17 3BS
0370 333 1181 | www.english-heritage.org.uk

OWNED BY ENGLISH HERITAGE

Built in the late 12th century by either William le Gros or (more likely) Baldwin of Bethune, the first fortification on the site was a wooden keep that was later converted to stone. The castle stands atop a tall mound controlling the strategically important Roman road that runs from Maidstone to the coast. In 1401 the estate was sold to provide a ransom for the release of Baron Grey of Ruthin, who had been captured by Owain Glyndŵr. By the end of the 18th century the castle was reported as being in a state of disrepair.

Tamworth Castle, Staffordshire

Holloway, Ladybank, Tamworth, Staffordshire, B79 7NA
01827 709626 | www.tamworthcastle.co.uk

OWNED BY TAMWORTH BOROUGH COUNCIL

Although the site has been fortified since Anglo-Saxon times, the current Norman motte-and-bailey castle dates from the 11th century. Added to and extended over the centuries, it includes a keep with a 12th-century gate tower, a 13th-century three-storey residential north range and a 17th-century Jacobean south range, all linked by an oak timbered Great Hall dating from the 15th century. During the English Civil War, the castle was captured by Parliamentary forces after a brief siege. Between the 17th and 19th centuries the castle had several different owners, before being bought at auction by Tamworth Corporation. It opened as a museum in 1899.

Thirlwall Castle, Northumberland

Thirlwall, Pennine Way, Brampton, CA8 7HL
www.northumberlandnationalpark.org.uk/
things-to-do/get-active-outdoors/walking/
walking-routes/thirlwall-castle-walk

MANAGED BY NORTHUMBERLAND NATIONAL PARK AUTHORITY

Built in the 12th century using stones from nearby
Hadrian's Wall, Thirlwall Castle was once the ancestral
home of the Thirlwall family. In 1485, Sir Percival Thirlwall
of Thirlwall Castle was killed at the Battle of Bosworth
Field; he was King Richard III's standard-bearer, and
sources claim that he held the colours high even after his
legs had been cut from under him. The castle fell into
disrepair some time in the 18th century, and in 1999 the
Northumberland National Park Authority took over
management of the site.

Thornbury Castle, Gloucestershire

Castle Street, Thornbury, Gloucestershire, BS35 1HH
01454 281182 | www.thornburycastle.co.uk

PRIVATELY OWNED

An impressive, well preserved 14th-century Tudor country
house as opposed to a defensive fortress, the castle was
built on the site of a 10th-century manor house. Work
began on the castle in 1511 as the planned home for
Edward Stafford, 3rd Duke of Buckingham. The Duke
was later beheaded for high treason by his relation King
Henry VIII in 1521 and the castle was seized by the King,
who stayed there on his honeymoon tour with Anne Boleyn.
The castle fell into ruin after the English Civil War of the
17th century before being restored by the Howard family
in the 19th century. Since then the castle has been a
private home and acclaimed restaurant before
becoming a hotel.

Tintagel Castle, Cornwall

Castle Road, Tintagel, Cornwall, PL34 0HE
01840 770328 | www.english-heritage.org.uk

OWNED BY ENGLISH HERITAGE

The site upon which Tintagel Castle stands was in use long before the castle was erected, with evidence of mining from Roman times. By the 5th century, Tintagel was a stronghold of Cornish kings. The association with the legends of King Arthur stem from the 10th-century tales of Geoffrey of Monmouth, whose 'History of Britain' suggests it as the birthplace of Arthur. Other legends claim that Tintagel is the site of Arthur's Camelot. It is thought that the current Tintagel Castle was the work of Richard, Earl of Cornwall (brother to King Henry III). Richard owned the site from about 1234, although it appears that the castle was not in use for long, as the hall was roofless by the mid-14th century.

Jo Jones / shutterstock.com

Tonbridge Castle, Tonbridge, Kent

Castle Street, Tonbridge, Kent, TN9 1BG
01732 770929 | www.tonbridgecastle.org

OWNED BY TONBRIDGE AND MALLING BOROUGH COUNCIL

Built by Richard Fitz Gilbert shortly after the Norman Conquest of England, Tonbridge Castle guards the crossing of the River Medway. In 1088 the castle was besieged by King William II. After holding out for two days, it fell; the king retaliated by burning both the castle and the town to the ground. Rebuilt in stone some years later by the de Clare family, the castle was further reinforced during the 13th century and in 1295 a stone wall was built around the town. The castle stood empty between the 16th and the late 18th century. In 1900 the site was purchased by the local council, who have carried out an extensive programme of restoration.

Totnes Castle, Devon

Castle Street, Totnes, Devon TQ9 5NU
01803 864406 | www.english-heritage.org.uk

OWNED BY ENGLISH HERITAGE

Built by one of William the Conqueror's lieutenants, Juhel of Totnes, shortly after the Norman Conquest of England, this early motte-and-bailey type fortification started life as an earthen mound topped by a wooden palisade. Constructed to control strategic crossings and sites, the castle occupies a commanding position guarding the approach to three valleys. Extensive remodelling in the 13th and 14th centuries created a circular stone keep atop the motte, surrounded by a curtain wall. Following the Wars of the Roses the castle fell into disrepair, although it is still considered to be one of the best-preserved examples of a Norman motte-and-bailey castle in the country.

Tower of London, Central London

London, EC3N 4AB
020 3166 6000 | www.hrp.org.uk/tower-of-london

OWNED BY HISTORIC ROYAL PALACES

Victorious at the Battle of Hastings on 14th October 1066, the invading William the Conqueror spent the rest of the year fortifying key strategic positions across southern England. At the time, London was the largest town in England and centre of governance with a prosperous port. The Normans needed to establish control over the settlement and demonstrate their dominance; hence the Tower of London was begun. Integrating the existing Roman town walls into its structure, the earliest phase would have been enclosed by a ditch and defended by a timber palisade, with accommodation for William. Most of the early Norman castles were constructed in wood, but by the end of the 11th century many had been rebuilt using stone. In 1087 work began on the White Tower, the earliest stone keep to be built in England. Around 1240, Henry III made the Tower his home, whitewashing the walls, extending the grounds and adding a great hall; the Normans called it La Tour Blanche, or the White Tower. Since then the tower has been used as a home for kings and queens, a royal mint, treasury, prison and royal zoo. Today it houses the Crown Jewels and the Royal Ravens.

ENTRY TO THE TRAITORS' GATE

Tutbury Castle, Staffordshire

Castle Street, Burton upon Trent, Tutbury,
Staffordshire, DE13 9JF
01283 812129 | tutburycastle.com

OWNED BY DUCHY OF LANCASTER

One of the seats of the noble de Ferrers family, Tutbury
Castle was first recorded in 1071, shortly after the
Norman Conquest of England. The castle was destroyed
by Prince Edward in 1264 after the rebellion of Robert de
Ferrers, 6th Earl of Derby. Apart from the 12th-century
chapel, today's ruins date from the 14th and 15th centuries
when the castle was rebuilt. Mary Queen of Scots was
imprisoned at Tutbury during the 16th century.
Destroyed and rebuilt several times over the centuries, it
suffered further damage during the English Civil War of
1642–46, and lapsed into ruin.

Tynemouth Castle, Tyne and Wear

Pier Road, Tynemouth, North Shields, Tyne and Wear,
NE30 4BZ
0191 257 1090 | www.english-heritage.org.uk

OWNED BY ENGLISH HERITAGE

Tynemouth Castle's moated castle-towers, gatehouse and
keep are all integrated within the ruins of a Benedictine
priory, which itself was founded early in the 7th century.
In AD 651 Oswin, King of Deira, was murdered and his
body was brought to Tynemouth for burial, the first of
three kings to be buried at the castle. Destroyed in a
Danish raid, a new monastery based on the Benedictine
discipline was established in about 1090, which lasted
until it was dissolved by Henry VIII. In 1539, the site was
transformed into a royal castle with gun emplacements
built to counter the threat of Spanish invasion.

Upnor Castle, Kent

Upnor Road, Rochester, Kent, ME2 4XG
01634 718742 | www.english-heritage.org.uk

OWNED BY ENGLISH HERITAGE

This rare example of an Elizabethan artillery fort was
begun in 1559 to protect the Royal Navy warships being
built and repaired at Chatham dockyards. After the
Dutch sailed right past it and destroyed thirteen English
ships at anchor, the defences of Chatham were revised in
1668. In the decades that followed, new, more powerful
forts were built farther down the Medway, effectively
making the castle redundant and forcing its repurposing
as a munitions store. Even so, it continued to be used
by the military until 1945, at which point it was declared
a museum.

Walmer Castle, Kent

Kingsdown Road, Walmer, Deal, Kent, CT14 7LJ
01304 364288 | www.english-heritage.org.uk

OWNED BY ENGLISH HERITAGE

One of many defensive structures commissioned by
Henry VIII to protect England's coast from foreign
invasion, Walmer Castle was one of the most advanced
military structures of its time. One of three forts
constructed to protect the Downs (an area of safe
anchorage off the Kent coast), Walmer's only taste of
action was during the English Civil War, when in 1648 it
surrendered to Parliamentary forces after a three-week
siege. Inhabited by the Duke of Wellington in his role as
Lord Warden of the Cinque Ports, it was here that the
hero of Waterloo died in 1852.

Warkworth Castle, Northumberland

Castle Terrace, Warkworth, Morpeth, Northumberland, NE65 0UJ
01665 711423 | www.english-heritage.org.uk

OWNED BY ENGLISH HERITAGE

Built after the Norman Conquest of England, Warkworth Castle occupies a loop of the River Coquet, less than a mile from England's north-east coast. The initial motte-and-bailey timber castle was rebuilt in stone during the Anglo-Scottish Wars, and in 1332 it ended up in the hands of the influential Percy family, eventually becoming one of their chief baronial castles. Unfortunately, the castle went into decline some time in the early 17th century, and was further damaged in the English Civil War, probably by Parliamentarian forces. By the 18th century the castle was in a complete state of disrepair, and it wasn't until the mid-19th century that some minor restoration work was carried out.

Warwick Castle, Warwickshire

Warwick, Warwickshire, CV34 6AH
0370 333 1181 | www.warwick-castle.com

OPERATED BY MERLIN ENTERTAINMENTS

Built shortly after the Norman Conquest of England in 1068 as a motte-and-bailey fortification, Warwick Castle occupies a once strategically important loop of the River Avon. In the 12th century the original wooden castle was rebuilt and fortified further during the Hundred Years War. In 1604 James VI and I granted the castle to Sir Fulke Greville, who lavished vast sums of money on modernising the castle to create a comfortable country house from the crumbling ruins of the medieval fortress. It was owned by the Greville family until 1978 when it was bought by the Tussauds Group.

Westenhanger Castle, Kent

Stone Street, Westenhanger, Hythe, Kent, CT21 4HX
01303 261068 | www.westenhangercastle.co.uk

OWNED BY KENT CASTLE LTD

The de Criol family were responsible for building the fortified manor house on the site in 1343, and it remained with the family until the War of the Roses when Sir Thomas de Criol was beheaded. Strengthened in response to threats of attack from France during the 14th century, in 1588 Queen Elizabeth used the castle as the command centre for troops who were to defend the south coast from the Spanish Armada. By the mid-17th century it was one of the largest houses in Kent, however shortly after this it started to fall into disrepair. Recent renovation work by the Forge family have reversed many decades of neglect, and today the castle is a fantastic wedding and event venue.

Whittington Castle, Shropshire

Castle Street, Whittington, Oswestry, Shropshire,
SY11 4DF
01691 662500 | www.whittingtoncastle.co.uk

OWNED BY WHITTINGTON CASTLE PRESERVATION FUND

The original Norman motte-and-bailey fortification was
rebuilt in the 13th century to include a stone curtain wall,
inner bailey and outer gatehouse with a 42-foot-long
drawbridge. As a castle of the Welsh Marches, it was built
on the border of Wales and England and provided
excellent views towards Offa's Dyke, over which Welsh
raiders frequently invaded. Although added to and
improved in the early 14th century, the castle gradually
fell into disrepair and by 1392 it was declared to be
'utterly in ruins'.

Wigmore Castle, Herefordshire

Wigmore, Leominster, Herefordshire, HR6 9UB
0370 333 1181 | www.english-heritage.org.uk

OWNED BY ENGLISH HERITAGE

Under the ownership of the powerful Mortimer family,
the original Norman wooden castle was rebuilt in stone
in the late 12th century and further enhanced throughout
the 13th century, thus creating one of the most important
and striking medieval fortresses in the Welsh Marches.
In the years that followed, conflict in the troubled border
areas calmed, eventually rendering such fortresses obsolete
and the Mortimer family moved their administrative centre
from Wigmore to Ludlow. Slighted during the English
Civil War, the castle fell into decay and eventual ruin.

Wilton Castle, Herefordshire

Wilton, Ross-on-Wye, Herefordshire, HR9 6AD
01989 565759 | www.wiltoncastle.eclipse.co.uk

OWNED BY MR AND MRS PARSLOW
NOT OPEN TO THE PUBLIC

Originally a Norman motte-and-bailey fortification, Wilton Castle was rebuilt in local sandstone during the 12th century by the powerful de Longchamps family. By the 16th century the military importance of Wilton had diminished, and when a more comfortable residence was required, a new manor house was built into the fabric of the castle. During the English Civil War, the then owner Sir John Brydges refused to support either side; this outraged local Royalists, and one Sunday morning whilst he was attending church, they burned the house down. A more modern manor was built in the 19th century, which remains a residence today.

Winchester Castle, Hampshire

Castle Avenue, Winchester, Hampshire, SO23 8UJ
01962 846476 | www.visitwinchester.co.uk/great-hall

OWNED BY HAMPSHIRE COUNTY COUNCIL

Built in 1067, just a year after the Norman Conquest of England, Winchester Castle was one of the grandest fortresses in England and initially served as the main seat of government before that was transferred to London. Rebuilt in stone and flint by Henry III, the royal apartments were further extended by Edward II. Little remains from that early period, as after the English Civil War in 1646 Oliver Cromwell ordered its destruction. Today, only Henry III's Great Hall survives intact, attached to which is a small museum detailing the history of Winchester. The Round Table of Arthurian legend can be seen on a wall in the Great Hall.

Windsor Castle, Berkshire

Windsor, Berkshire, SL4 1NJ
0303 123 7304 | www.royalcollection.org.uk/visit/
windsorcastle

OWNED BY ROYAL COLLECTION TRUST

Now the largest inhabited castle in the world and the oldest in continuous occupation, Windsor was originally built by William the Conqueror to secure Norman dominance around London, and to oversee a strategically important part of the River Thames. The typical earth and wood motte-and-bailey structure was gradually replaced with stone fortifications over time. In 1175 Henry II strengthened the defences and added the first of the royal apartments; he even planted a vineyard! Over the centuries, almost every king and queen of England has lavished funds on Windsor, adding to and rebuilding this now luxurious royal palace.

Wolvesey Castle, Hampshire

34 College Walk, Winchester, Hampshire, SO23 9NF
0370 333 1181 | www.english-heritage.org.uk

OWNED BY ENGLISH HERITAGE

Commissioned by the Bishop of Winchester, Henry of Blois, and built between 1130 and 1140, this early Norman keep-and-bailey castle was quickly extended and further fortified during the Civil War between Queen Matilda and King Stephen known as The Anarchy. Once a supremely important building, in July 1554 it hosted the wedding breakfast of Queen Mary and Philip II of Spain before they left for their wedding ceremony at nearby Winchester Cathedral. Destroyed by the Parliamentarians during the English Civil War in 1646, the chapel is the only substantial remnant of the original castle. The chapel and castle remains were then incorporated into the 'new' bishop's palace, which was built in 1684.

Image credits